Make it Happen

Make it Happen

A Practical Handbook for **Team Leaders, Project Managers** and **Facilitators** to Build, Facilitate and Repair **High Performance Teams**

Tony White

Library and Archives Canada Cataloguing in Publication

White, Tony, 1960-
        Make it happen : a practical guide for team leaders, project managers and facilitators to build, facilitate and repair high-performance teams / Tony White.

Includes bibliographical references.
ISBN 0-9737613-0-X

        1. Teams in the workplace. 2. Group facilitation. I. Title.

HD66.W49 2005   658.4'036   C2005-901289-7

Make it Happen
A Practical Handbook for Team Leaders, Project Managers and Facilitators to Build, Facilitate and Repair High Performance Teams

Published by:
Golfside Publications
103 Pinnacle Trail
Aurora, Ontario
Canada
L4G 7G7

Printed in Canada
10 9 8 7 6 5 4 3 2 1

Acknowledgements

This book could not have been written without the support and contribution of a number of key people both in my business and personal life.

Richard Wigley from PMI who designed the Facilitation Skills Workshop and introduced me to many of the concepts detailed in Chapters 1 and 2 of this book. Jack Asgar of PMI whose years of wisdom have been crucial in shaping not only this book but also my training career. The team at PMCI, that helped me with the early editions. Rob Henderson, friend and colleague, who introduced to me the concept of the team pyramid. My mother Ivy and late father, Norman, who have stood with me my entire life — whatever my passion was. My children, Lauren and Blake, who provide me with perspective. My life partner, Elaine, for believing in and pushing me get "myself in gear" to finish this book.

Contents

The Need for **High Performance** Teams

What is in this book for **you**?

Do you suffer from any of the following?

* **Demotivated team members, leading to poor performance levels**

* **Frustration because your team members are having problems meeting deadlines**

* **Feelings of helplessness, as you try to figure out how to get your team back on track**

* **Lack of communication between your team members, resulting in all of the above problems**

As a Team Leader you are inundated with articles, books, workshops and on-line resources that explain how to make your team more effective. If you are like most leaders, you probably take one or two key ideas from these resources and apply them directly to your team back on the job.

What you can expect from this book:

✳ **A template to help you build, or rebuild your team after a merger, acquisition, reorganization or downsizing process**

✳ **A template to help the Team Leader or Project Manager who has just been promoted to leading a high-performance team**

✳ **Numerous, simple yet highly effective tips and techniques to help you facilitate highly participative, input-driven team meetings and discussions resulting in higher levels of team motivation and productivity**

✳ **A detailed set of coaching activities that can be implemented by you when faced with a demotivated and/or underachieving team**

The focus of this book is to help Team Leaders, reap the benefits of having a collection of individuals work together in a highly effective, productive manner in order to meet business goals and objectives.

The primary application of the skills and strategies in this book are for "natural" teams – that is, a collection of individuals that make up a business unit, which reports to a Team Leader. In many organizations, the term "Team Leader" is synonymous with the Supervisor or Manager position.

Examples of natural teams would include a small printing company, where the five-person team might consist of an account executive, office manager, customer service representative, and a bookkeeper —who all report to a director. While in a large manufacturing operation, the natural team could consist of 25 production workers, and two lead hands, all reporting to a supervisor. In both cases, the Team Leader (whether called a director or a supervisor or any other title) is accountable for the business activities and results of the team that reports to him/her.

However, if you do not lead a "natural" team, this book will help the Project Manager in a matrix environment, where team members (that do not directly report to the Project Manager) are pulled together, for a pre-defined period to create a product or service.

A good example would be a large service based organization where individuals are asked to join a temporary team in order to improve customer relations, for example, and be accountable, temporarily to the Project Leader or Manager.

Furthermore, if you are asked to facilitate a task force, steering committee, focus group, strategic planning initiative, legislated committee (e.g., Health and Safety Team) or some other special "team" that requires a group of people to work together toward a common goal, this book will detail the core activities that are required to build, facilitate, and if necessary, repair such a team.

No matter what type of business-related team you lead, this book is designed to help you take your team's motivation and performance to the next level – that is, to the level of what I refer to as a high-performance team.

Do you currently lead a High-Performance Team?

The most critical person in this equation is you - the Team Leader – the person who is accountable for building, maintaining and when necessary, repairing the team when its focus is lost.

During the past ten years, I have used the questionnaire on page 17 to help Team Leaders quickly gauge whether or not their team would be considered High Performance. Before you read on, take five minutes now and complete the questionnaire— it will provide you with a vivid illustration of your team's current state.

> **My definition of a high-performance team is simple– it is a team of people that consistently meets and then exceeds business expectations, is highly motivated and whose attrition rate is minimal.**

What part of the book will be most useful to you?

This book is written as three distinct and standalone chapters. Although there are occasional cross-references to other chapters, each chapter can be easily read and understood *without having to read the others.*

Therefore

If you are an experienced Team Leader who is having trouble motivating your team or are experiencing frustration with your team's inability to meet performance expectations, *go directly to Chapter 3.*

If you are a Team Leader who needs strategies and skills to help you facilitate participative, input-driven team meetings and discussions, *go directly to Chapter 2.*

If you are a new Team Leader with little experience in the start-up phases of a new team, or have just experienced a merger, acquisition, reorganization or downsizing process, *read the book from start to finish.*

Chapter 1 helps the Team Leader understand the team maturation process and outlines the macro-level strategies that are necessary to successfully build the foundation of a high-performance team.

Research and practical experience has proven that the Team Leader who takes a proactive, assertive approach (with a new or realigned team) will have a much greater chance of creating and then maintaining a high-performance team.

The first part of the chapter provides you with a brief overview of the team development process; the second part focuses on the macro-level strategies that need to be initiated by you – the Team Leader.
Chapter 2 outlines the discussion skills (i.e. facilitation skills) that a

Team Leader must possess in order to maintain a participative, motivating and productive environment with a work team. My experience indicates that the Team Leader's ability to facilitate both informal team discussions as well as more formal input-driven meetings, e.g. a monthly planning meeting, is critical to the maintenance of a high-performance team.

Research and practical experience has taught me that successful Team Leaders have a "method to their facilitation madness" and that *they facilitate well by design, not by default.*

Chapter 3 examines some of the most common reasons that teams run into trouble and then outlines the micro-level coaching skills and strategies required by the Team Leader to get the team back on track. Even the most dedicated, well-intentioned and competent Team Leader will, at some point, face the daunting challenge of having to decide on a remedial course of action for a team that is currently not reaching its objectives.

My path to this book

Why did I feel compelled to write a book? During the past twenty years I have led workshops for literally thousands of Team Leaders across Canada, the US and parts of Europe, with the intent of providing them with the skills and strategies that will help them become better at leading teams. During that time, I too have been a Team Leader, both in a post-secondary educational environment and as a founding partner in Practical Management of Canada Inc.

Why do I bother with these details? Because, after graduating from university, I thought I was ready to tackle the challenge of Team Management — I figured that with a Masters Degree in Sport Management and having played team sports most of my life, I had all the equipment necessary to succeed!

Apparently, I was mistaken...

I had just began working as a Coordinator of Continuing Education (i.e. adult night school) at Seneca College in North York, Ontario, Canada. In the subsequent eight years of employment at Seneca, I moved around to a number of campuses, working for different managers and carrying out different job functions, but always focused on the same end results — to help adult learners learn.

During that time, I had to lead a number of "teams" ranging from part-time faculty committees to focus groups comprised of adult students. Although I felt that most of these experiences were successful, I rarely had any real plan behind what I did as a Team Leader. I observed how other coordinators and more senior level managers led their teams and their corresponding differences in approach — some resulting in extremely motivated and productive team members, others resulting in poor outcomes and startling attrition rates.

The culmination of these early experiences made me ask, "What is it that effective Team Leaders do to truly motivate, facilitate and lead a high performance team?" As I have been unable to find any literature that outlines these skills and strategies in a format that is practical, easy to read and user-friendly, I decided to embark upon this challenge.

I hope you enjoy the ride...

High Performance

Team Questionnnaire™

The following 20 questions will help you determine your current effectiveness in leading and creating a productive and motivating team environment with your team members.

Answer each question honestly and score yourself appropriately on your current behaviour rather than the behaviour *that you believe* you should be engaging in.

Scoring Scale (Place the number in the box located at each question)

1 I never or very rarely demonstrate this behavior
2 I occasionally demonstrate this behavior when the situation calls for it
3 I demonstrate this behavior on a regular basis when the situation calls for it
4 I demonstrate this behavior consistently

☐ 1. When performance or project goals change, I proactively clarify them with my team members.

☐ 2. The roles of our team members are well defined and are continually reviewed and updated as the department or team evolves.

☐ 3. Work procedures are detailed and, where appropriate, created with input from the team members.

☐ 4. I ensure that the links between team members' personal performance goals, team goals, department goals and organizational goals, are crystal clear.

☐ 5. Formal and informal teambuilding activities are carried out with the team.

☐ 6. I explain why our team is structured the way it is and give opportunities to comment and/or improve upon it.

☐ 7. During team meetings, I ensure that we assertively attack the problems – not other team members.

☐ 8. When leading team discussions, I consciously try to recognize the contributions that team members make.

☐ 9. I actively listen to other team members and avoid downplaying their viewpoint, if it's different from mine.

☐ 10. I actively try to empathize with team members' issues, even if I do not personally agree with them.

☐ 11. If I notice others are not participating in team meetings, I try to encourage them to get involved in a meaningful manner.

12. When team members get angry or frustrated, I try to help them work through the issue to achieve a positive outcome.

13. We create ground rules or behavioral operating guidelines to be used when team meetings and discussions go off-track.

14. Where possible, I coach when team members struggle to meet their performance or project goals.

15. I monitor and effectively use the agreed upon communication methods and channels that have been established by our team.

16. I teach team members the best techniques and/or methodologies to communicate effectively with me.

17. I actively seek feedback from team members in relation to my leadership effectiveness.

18. I attempt to deal with inter-team conflicts and disagreements in an efficient, non-confrontational manner.

19. I realize that trust is an integral part of team effectiveness and I actively look for ways to build trust between the team members.

20. I realize that trust is an integral part of team leadership, and I actively look for ways to build trust with my individual team members.

Now total your score for the twenty questions.

Total Score

TEAM EFFECTIVENESS Total Score

Interpreting the Results

If you scored 60 to 80 points

You have a good grasp of what it takes to be a strong Team Leader. You appreciate the importance of a solid team foundation, which encompasses goal setting, role clarification and clarity of procedures and policies.
Questions 1 through 6 are the best indicators of this competence.

You have a strong ability to both lead and contribute to team meetings and discussions and have a good balance of both advocating your viewpoint as well as listening to others.
Questions 7 through 13 through are the best indicators of your contribution to meetings.

Finally, your ability to work through team conflict is excellent.
Questions 14 through 20 are the best indicators of your abilities in this area.

If you scored 59 points or lower

There is some room for improvement in what it takes to be an effective Team Leader. Part of the challenge might be due to "environmental factors" such as insufficient resources to do the job adequately or lack of senior management support. You have a basic understanding of the importance of having a solid team foundation, which encompasses goal setting, role clarification and clarity of procedures and policies.

Questions 1 through 6 are the best indicators of this competence and may be an area to target for enhancing your personal success in this area.

There are opportunities to enhance your ability to facilitate and contribute to team meetings and discussions, and realign your balance of both advocating your viewpoints as well as listening to others.

Questions 7 through 13 are the best indicators of your contributions and could be an area to target for enhancing your personal success.

Finally, your ability to work through team conflict can be strengthened.

Questions 14 through 20 are the best indicators of your ability in this sphere and may be a target for enhancing your personal success in this area.

1 **Building** the Foundation for a **High Performance** Team

Understanding the Practical Implications of **Team Dynamics**

This chapter outlines the macro-level strategies (detailed instructions on how to implement these strategies are outlined in Chapter 3: Repairing Teams When Things Go Wrong) and critical activities that the Team Leader must consider and implement when building or rebuilding a work team. Team Leaders who take a proactive, assertive approach with a new or realigned team will have a much greater chance of creating and then maintaining a high-performance team.

The first part of this chapter provides the reader with a brief overview of the team maturation process while the second part focuses on what the Team Leader needs to do in order to successfully build the foundation for a high-performance team.

FORM-STORM-NORM-PERFORM Revisited

Before a Team Leader can effectively lead a team towards a set of business objectives, he/she needs to have a clear picture of how a group of individuals will, eventually, transform into the entity that I refer to as a High Performance Team.

The team development model that originally was researched and written about in 1965 by Tuckman[1], was, and still is, one of the most comprehensive studies of the dynamics of people in teams. Most team practitioners and Organizational Development (O.D.) specialists have adopted this model as the basis for understanding effective team building.

The next section will briefly detail what behaviour you will observe in each of the four stages of team maturation – remember this is based on the academic influence of the model that will not always reflect the reality of the business environment you work in. Therefore, this discussion will be followed by *what actually happens* with most teams in a business environment, and then completed with a list of *what practically needs to happen* to build the foundation of a high-performance team.

STAGES OF **Team Development**

Although not as predictable as we would like, all teams, whether natural or project based go through a maturation process. With project based teams that typically last only weeks or months, the maturation process still occurs but it tends to be quicker and more obvious as the time lines are compressed. Human behaviour being what it is, the stages of growth will tend to be somewhat fleeting and obscure with indicators ranging from subtle to overt. Nonetheless, as a group of individuals develops into a mature team, a pattern of development emerges.

During this unpredictable maturation process, it is critical that a Team Leader is both alert to the symptoms of growth, or lack thereof, and prepared to take the actions necessary to move the team

1. B.W. Tuckman, "Developmental Sequence in Small Groups," Psychological Bulletin, 1965, Vol. 63, No. 6, 384-399

through the stages. The Team Leader must smooth out the bumps, obstacles and barriers that will spring up along the way.

However, in reality, the team's development does not follow a linear progression — meaning that many individuals and teams will move back and forth through these stages depending upon numerous factors.

STAGE 1 - Testing (Forming)

Remember back to the days when you were a new member of a team…

How did you feel when you took a seat in the meeting room with your new teammates? Excited? Nervous? Fearful? Blasé? Put upon? Pressured? What were your thoughts about the other people who would be there? What were the unknowns about the whole experience? What role were you going to have to play?

Multiply the myriad of questions and concerns by the number of people on the team and you have a fair picture of the collective state of mind that exists in the early stage of a team's development. Individuals coming together for the first time in a business entity, even if they know each other, will all have personal concerns about the developing relationships, the most notable of which will be, "How do I fit in with this team?" This stage is a collection of everybody's past experiences, which range from extremely positive to extremely negative, in dealing with new team situations. Some individuals are lively and outgoing, others are quiet and observant, some congregate only with those they know and others move quickly to make new acquaintances.

As the team forms, the "feeling out" process begins with people broadening their range of contacts, seeking to discover attitudes, values, approachability and points of commonality. Gradually, people begin to form judgments as to the nature of the team and their involvement in it.

Outwardly, the team seems to be functioning well and people have quickly reached a level of comfort and camaraderie with each other. This condition, however, can be superficial since it is the product of socializing behaviour that might be irrespective of the team's business purpose. As team issues such as inadequate resources, lack of management support etc., begin to arise, the comfort level can disappear.

Thus, *it is critical that the Team Leader ensures that early team activities are a good mixture of social, personal and business experience so that the reality of doing business is not lost in excessive socializing and "feel-good" team building activities.* See Chapter 2 for more information about developing appropriate team building activities.

STAGE 2 - Infighting (Storming)

The desire for power and control by various team members begins to materialize and informal leadership issues (e.g. who knows who? is someone getting preferential treatment? etc.) emerge as concerns about performance, expertise, and influence become evident.

Alliances can form and certain people become significant players. Leadership styles will be observed, privately evaluated and perhaps challenged in overt or subtle ways.

During this stage, the team is deciding how it is going to operate. Which rules of conduct will govern its behaviour and to what extent are these rules unbreakable? Too often, the mechanism for maintaining appropriate conduct and behaviour is allowed to evolve rather than being planned, supported and reinforced by the Team Leader. Critical behaviour and team rules are tested. What happens to "delinquents"? How are rule violators handled? What happens if business deliverables are not completed? How are conflicts dealt with?

This stage can be the make or break period for any team. The inability to successfully confront these issues and circumstances leaves a permanent scar from which the team might not recover. Conversely, open and direct confrontation with these issues and their successful resolution has immense developmental value.

The skill of the Team Leader can well be severely tested during this stage. While there are no pat answers, *it is critical that operating rules and controls be established early, and that issues be confronted immediately.* It is not unusual for major changes in team membership, operating rules, and perhaps even the charter or overall purpose of the team to change during this stage.

STAGE 3 - Creating (Norming)

Having worked through their most difficult period (for now), team members are now ready and willing to make the team successful by reaching its goals and objectives. Unanimous commitment and involvement is important at this stage because individual agendas and preoccupation with unrelated issues can hinder the team's growth.

The quality and intensity of members' interactions become paramount as the team begins to encourage individual contributions and creates its own personality with respect to communications; dealing with new ideas and options, and evaluating the economy and effectiveness of its actions. At this stage, growth is measured by the team's ability to handle problems and tasks with creativity and flexibility. Evidence of progress, support from upper levels of management and patience by all is critical, as this stage can take a considerable amount of time.

Support, reinforcement and counseling are the key roles of the Team Leader during this stage. Encouraging creativity, risk-taking, flexibility; using mistakes as opportunities to learn and grow; counseling individuals who are not pulling their weight or are reluctant to express themselves; recommending external resources and sources of expertise — all are critical functions of the Team Leader.

STAGE 4 · Mature Bonding (Performing)

Rapport and a sense of togetherness directed at team performance are the primary characteristics of this stage. Team members extend themselves for each other and for the team. They compliment each other's competencies—one member's strengths balance another's weaknesses. Formal rules and controls can relax somewhat as members' comfort levels allow for more informality and spontaneity. Team roles are clear; areas of expertise and contribution have been identified. Pride in progress and performance is evident and spills out beyond the team. Formal and informal communication links are established to spread the word of the team's accomplishments. Outside recognition becomes important as a way of verifying what the team knows they have accomplished.

The Team Leader's role has evolved into an "Obstacle Removal Specialist [2]", assertively being on the lookout for obstacles — both in the team environment and the larger business environment — that have the potential to derail the team from meeting their goals and objectives. Obstacles, such as unforeseen changes in customer expectations, technology advances, senior management interference, to name a few, must be dealt with effectively and immediately so that the team can maintain its motivation and focus on the job at hand.

---

2. Keeping with the trend of creating titles that sound impressive—e.g. —Gas Station Attendant is a now a *Petroleum Distribution Agent.*

FORM-STORM-NORM-PERFORM-The Reality

Over the past twenty years of working with literally thousands of teams in business, government, and educational settings, the applicability of this model as I have explained it, must be revisited. I am assuming that Tuckman, in his original writings never intended for the model to be viewed as four, distinct, equal parts of a pie: 25 percent of the time spent in forming, 25 percent in storming, 25 percent in norming, and 25 percent in performing (see Figure 1.1). Although academically sound, *this model needs to be used as a filter to truly understand what dynamics occur within most teams.*

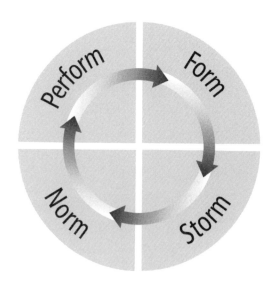

Figure 1.1 – The Original Team Model–The Common Perception

As can be seen in Figure 1.2, very little time and/or intensive effort is spent in the forming stage, thereby resulting in an extra-ordinary expenditure of time and energy during the storming stage. When the storming stage becomes too dysfunctional, there is usually some sort of team "shake-up" resulting in team mandates being changed, team members being transferred or Team Leaders being fired. Furthermore, the norming and then performing stages are correspondingly smaller than in the original model.

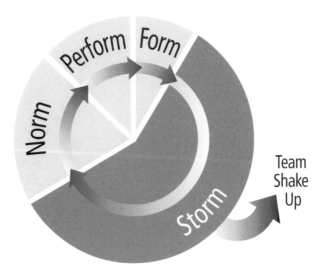

Figure 1.2 - What happens in reality...

What does this mean on a practical, day-to-day basis with a team?

Human nature dictates that, typically, people want to jump directly to problem solving and solution generation as quickly as possible. The Team Leader is no exception. Hence, very little effort is expended in the forming stage or, as I call it, the foundation building stage.

This is most commonly due to:

✳ **The Team Leader being unaware of the importance of this stage in helping to build for the future**

✳ **The fact that it isn't a lot of fun working through foundation building activities**

✳ **The hard work seems to have little payback in the short-term**

Usually, team introductions are made at either a social outing or at a meeting to rally the troops and the team goals are communicated, and then teams are sent forth to work as a productive, cohesive and harmonious unit. Is it any wonder that many teams struggle and end up being disbanded or provided with career expanding opportunities?[3]

Because the intensity of effort has not been spent in the forming stage, numerous issues show up throughout the team's early life. This results in conflict, disagreement, and in most cases confusion about what the team is there to do, who is accountable for what, and the procedures that are to be followed. Hence, in many cases, the storming stage becomes monstrous and insurmountable.

As can be seen in Figure 1.2, if the storming stage gets intense enough, the team will be dismantled either by senior management or through team member's movement or attrition. Furthermore, if the team does actually survive the storming stage, the norming and performing stages might occur but, given the amount of time they spent psychologically beating each other up, members' sense of job satisfaction tends to be compromised. Hence, their willingness to be engaged in a similar team structure will be lessened. In addition, the Team Leader has to deal with the motivational fallout that is a net result of all of this confusion and frustration.

FORM-STORM-NORM-PERFORM... The Goal

If you've ever built a house, a dock, a cottage, etc. you would say that the most difficult, backbreaking work is building the foundation. Any building contractor will agree, without a doubt, that *the foundation is the most critical part of the building process.* If a solid foundation is not built, when the upper levels of the structure are

---

3. Career expansion sounds significantly better than being fired.

created and are faced with poor weather, shifting earth and natural disasters, the house will shift, crack and in the worse case scenario, collapse.

The building of a team's foundation is very similar in nature. If a strong foundation is not constructed, eventually the team will splinter, argue, sabotage or in the worse case scenario, be disbanded and fall apart. Look at the forming stage in Figure 1.3 as foundation building for a team's future success.

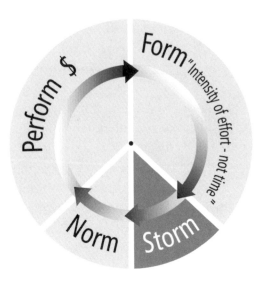

Figure 1.3 - The Goal

However, in the forming stage the concept of "intensity of effort, not time" must be examined, especially in light of a team that has emerged from an acquisition or merger.

Most Team Leaders, when they examine this model for the first time, remark:

"We do not have the time to spare that seemingly is required in the forming stage."

Depending on the type of team, its objectives and projected lifespan, the forming stage can be taken care of in a few hours if it is done efficiently. Therefore, when we talk about foundation building, it is not the time that the Team Leader has to invest — *it is the intensity of effort and the quality of the discussions that occur in the forming stage that will help the team move forward.*

> **My experience has shown that the majority of issues, which prevent a team from reaching its daily goals, tend to be related to the lack of preparation or intensity of effort spent up front with the team, during the foundation building process.**

Any model will conceptually differ from the reality of what happens in the business world.

If you have led a team that has been less than successful in reaching its objectives, think back to what you have just read. Did you spend the intensity of effort upfront building that foundation?

Therefore the question that arises is: *"What sort of things should I be practically doing in the forming stage to set my team up for success?"*

The Three Critical Foundation Building Activities

I have found the following activities to be essential in building the team's foundation for success. Experience shows that there is a greater likelihood of teams reaching their business objectives (i.e. the performing stage) in a timely, efficient manner if the Team Leader exerts the intensity of effort up-front to these activities. Furthermore, as a post-merger or acquisition team, these activities take on a greater significance due to fear, confusion and issues of job security experienced by team members.

Focused, Collective and Agreed Upon Goals

As teams evolve, so do the goals for which Team Leaders are accountable. Although any competent Team Leader understands that goal setting is an integral part of successful management, it is even more crucial after a merger or acquisition. Team members are unsure and in many cases downright frightened after a "re-org". A meeting that helps clarify the goals and, where possible, solicits the team members' input into the action plans that support the goals will go a long way to alleviate their fears — see Chapter 3 for more detailed information on goal setting.

If you are a Team Leader in a project based structure where the team has a pre-defined "shelf-life" and your team members report, in most cases, to a "natural" Team Leader as well, then this activity becomes even more pivotal as team members will have to juggle multiple goals and in many cases, multiple priorities. You must clearly articulate focused, collective and agreed-upon goals so that team members can fully understand what is expected of them in conjunction with their other daily priorities. For example, in many large manufacturing and design companies, team members are constantly being seconded on a part-time basis from their "natural" jobs to a special team for a preset period. During this time they are usually expected to maintain their daily work, thereby keeping their natural Team Leader happy while heavily contributing to their project team thereby keeping their other "Team Leader" happy. In this type of situation, *most successful Team Leaders make a concerted effort to sit down with the team member's "natural" team boss to discuss and agree upon priorities and goals* — thereby avoiding putting the team member in the middle of a "tug-of-war" game.

Clear Roles

Role ambiguity and confusion is particularly evident in team members after an organizational realignment. Conversely, a team that has worked together for a period of time and now has a new Team Leader with potentially different expectations can be disconcerting to say the least. What was once a clearly defined role might be totally reworked when two or more corporate cultures are suddenly merged or a new Team Leader is thrown into the mix.

A solid discussion, initiated by the Team Leader, in regards to each member's role is crucial to help focus people's energies and quickly ramp up productivity levels. Defining each member's new role —as well as one's own— also helps avoid duplication of effort and increases tolerance toward each other as members begin to realize that they are not the only ones struggling with this new entity (see Chapter 3 for more detailed information around role clarification).

Documented Procedures

As well as the change in roles, day-to-day procedures will change, in some cases dramatically, with any organizational realignment or when a new Team Leader joins the team. Processes that people have developed and followed for years can become obsolete overnight. Wherever possible, *the Team Leader must help the team members find the commonalities between the new processes with the old so that total helplessness and despondency are kept at bay.*

This is the one foundation activity where the team members (rather than senior levels of management), if experienced, can have significant input into the development of the new procedures that will be required to meet the team's changing and/or evolving roles and goals – *resulting in procedures that are actually adhered to and relevant to each team member.*

Summary

As can be seen in Figure 1.4, the result of not focusing on the foundation building activities can be devastating, not only to the entire team, but also to the Team Leader. Discussion around roles, goals and procedures will not only help the team move toward their business goals and, ultimately, higher levels of performance, but will also provide a certain amount of personal satisfaction in regards to the relationships with the other team members (See Figure 1.5). The role of a Team Leader is to assertively embrace and expedite these foundation-building activities with their team members and, during the first year, be prepared to revisit the foundational decisions on a regular basis as the team gradually evolves.

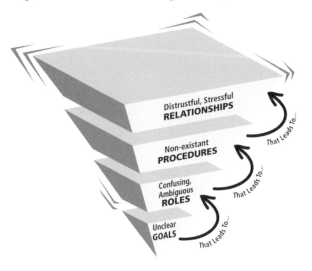

Figure 1.4 – When Foundation Building Activities Are Not Present

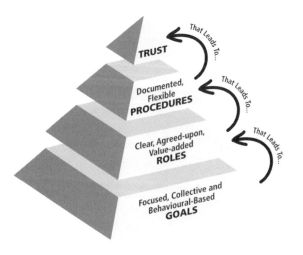

Figure 1.5 – The Results of Foundation Building

2 Maintenance of High Performance Teams

through Facilitated Discussions and Action Planning

The purpose of this chapter is to detail the discussion (i.e. facilitation) skills and strategies that a Team Leader must possess in order to maintain a participative, motivating and productive environment with a work team. My experience has shown that the Team Leader's ability to facilitate both informal team discussions as well as more formal, input-driven meetings, such as a monthly planning meeting, is critical to the maintenance of high-performing teams.

Research and practical experience has demonstrated that the most successful Team Leaders have an actual "method to their facilitation madness" and that they facilitate well by design, not by default.

Before we start… ice breaking and team building, or is it ice building and team breaking?

Prior to discussing the requisite skills and strategies required to facilitate productive, interactive team discussions and decisions, the concept of team building needs to be examined.

> "Team building is any activity that is carried out by a group of people that allows them to better understand both the issue at hand and each other for the purpose of reaching a business outcome more effectively and efficiently."

Teambuilding is a critical component of the foundation building or forming stage that was discussed in Chapter 1. Since the early 1970s, many authors turned business consultants have made thousands of dollars creating and selling books, games and activities designed to help Team Leaders "team build." The theory behind many of these "team builders" is that if you can get people talking, helping one another, and problem solving while engaged in an activity, usually unrelated to their business purpose, then these behaviours should spill over into their day-to-day business environment. Some authors will call these activities "icebreakers"[4]. For the purpose of this discussion I suggest that both team building and icebreaking are synonymous. With deeper analysis and discussion one can successfully argue that there are important differences between the two, but I have found that the two types of activities usually result in similar outcomes.

My definition of team building:

My experience has shown that the intent of many team building activities is quite sound. In other words, when the activity is designed, the goal is to get people to work well together, understand an issue more thoroughly and, in many cases, have some fun.

Let me make one point perfectly clear…I have no issue with the team having fun in the initial forming stages when people are trying to feel each other out (see Chapter #1 for more information on the Forming Stage).

Actually, I strongly encourage it. *However, it is equally critical that any team building activity must be seen as something that directly contributes to the business objectives of the team.* In many cases, the fun aspect of these activities ends up being the focal point of the entire activity — resulting in less than optimal outcomes.

4. Icebreakers are usually the term given to start-up activities at the beginning of workshops and seminars.

Case in point:

Row, Row, Row Your Boat …

In Toronto, Ontario, Canada[5], I recently attended a one-day workshop held near the airport in one of the local hotels. This workshop was entitled "Team Building Activities for Team Leaders." Always trying to enhance the training services that I offer, I attended this workshop to see what my competitors were promoting, and if any untapped wisdom was going unnoticed. I should have known by the price, $99, and the fact that we were in a room that held 150 people, that I might not be 100 percent satisfied with the day's outcome. The well spoken, immaculately dressed facilitator exclaimed, "We are going to jump right into our first team building activity that you can bring back and apply to your teams."

We were then told to reach under our chairs and find an envelope that was taped to the chair's underside. After searching around and navigating through pieces of gum and other assorted foreign matter, I found my envelope, opened it up, and removed a sheet of paper that read "Row, row, row your boat". The facilitator now explained that we needed to stand up and sing the song printed on our individual sheets of paper[6].

I didn't realize that there were four or five different songs scattered around the room ranging from "Row Your Boat" to "Jingle Bells". I am sure you can imagine the sound of 150 people singing five different songs scattered randomly around a room all at the same time. It was not a pleasant sound or sight, for that matter.

Eventually, you were asked to find the other poor souls who were singing the same song as you, and then told to cluster into a corner

5. One of the most competitive training and development markets in the world!

6. At this point I was tempted to nearly row, row, row to the parking lot and then all the way home!

of the room where you would sing in unison, or as much unison as a group of 20 to 25 tone deaf adults could muster.

You might be wondering - did all 150 people get up and sing? If you answered "no" you're right. However, by my count close to 95 percent of the people did get up and sing. [7] The important question is, did it add any value to the "team" and did they enjoy doing it? Definitely not. Transport this activity back to the workplace and if you're the Team Leader observing your group with their teeth gritted through their smiles, singing their songs, you could think, "This is great; we're starting to bond; we're starting to build a team."

What did people really think of this activity? They certainly didn't make their feelings publicly known until the first coffee break. Their comments ranged from "that was the most ridiculous activity I have ever done" to "he surely couldn't expect that I would bring that activity back to my work teams and actually use it?"

Must I remind you that the name of the workshop was "Team Building Activities for Team Leaders...."

> **Such an activity has the potential to not only undermine your credibility but to undermine the seriousness of the team concept itself.[8]**

As a warm-up activity at a Song Writers' Convention, or as a method to determine softball teams at the company's summer picnic this exercise might work. But as an activity to help a new team form, it fails miserably. Try implementing this activity during the first meeting with the team, and *it quickly becomes a teambreaker or an icebuilder.* It's one thing if I decide to waste my time, it's another thing if someone else wastes it for me and, in turn, makes me look foolish in front of my peers.

---

7. It never fails to amaze me what you can get adults to do under peer pressure!

8. In the 1970s and 1980s during the height of Total Quality Management (TQM), many a CEO was asked to cut and paste Sesame Street characters and create a collage with his team, all in the name of teambuilding!

Team Building and Motivation – A Potentially Inverse Relationship

Furthermore, the concept of team building is often prescribed as a way to correct poor team leadership - not consciously of course, but it happens daily in organizations worldwide.

For example, Bob, the Team Leader of a small team of IT specialists felt his team was in need of a motivational boost. On the rare occasions that Bob was around the office, he was often brusque, uncommunicative and ogre-like. Bob decided to hire a vendor that specialized in outdoor team building activities and arranges for a daylong offsite event. The team learned how to better communicate with each other, deal effectively with inter-team conflict and in general have a grand time. The external facilitator artfully took them through the day and helped them understand how the behaviour demonstrated that day, would foster greater teamwork and collaboration back at the job-site.

Had Bob been doing an effective job as a Team Leader, for the previous 364 days, and had he been willing to actively help the team apply the behaviour back on the job, then an increased motivation and productivity level might have resulted, as seen in Figure 2.1. Team building event with on-the-job follow-up.

However Bob, who expected the team building day to magically motivate his team to higher levels of productivity, actually observed poorer team dynamics and productivity compared to before the team building initiative (Figure 2.2). With the exception of a brief motivational spike right after the actual event, Bob saw a team of demotivated people who seemed to be going through the motions and, in general, were the antithesis of a high-performance team.

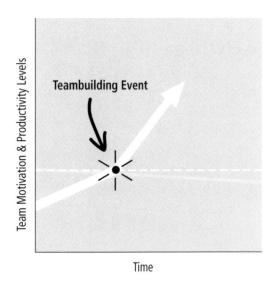

Figure 2.1. Team building event with on-the-job follow-up.

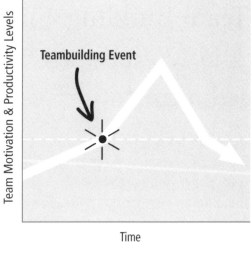

Figure 2.2 Team building event without on-the-job follow-up.

This result came about because the IT team members had greater expectations of each other, of Bob and of the work environment in which they functioned on a daily basis. The team-building day taught them how to do the "right stuff" but unfortunately the grim reality of their workplace quickly jolted them back into the real world. Their newfound motivation was, at best, fleeting and was soon replaced by apathy and disillusionment.

Having made all of these disparaging remarks around team building, let me emphatically state that such activities, either to help a team form more quickly or as a motivational tool for ongoing teams, can be very effective — providing the Team Leader carries out his/her role properly. If the Team Leader uses the strategies and techniques outlined in this chapter on a regular basis, then the team building process will be successful. *This is because the majority of the tools and strategies outlined in this book are in essence day-to-day team building activities that are built into a team's weekly operating environment.*

Team Building -
The Five Critical Criteria

Any team building activity should be created with the following five criteria kept in mind. I am not going to provide you with a list of team building activities, as the best of them are those that are directly related to the team's day-to-day business activities. If you want to use an activity that you have found in a book or on a website, use the following criteria as an *acid test* to ensure that the activity will achieve what you want.

1. Does the activity enable participants to talk with each other?

Because you expect this group of individuals to work as a team, it is critical that they are comfortable in conversing with each other and with you in an open, honest, effective manner. Therefore, one of the benchmarks of a successful activity is that it gets team members participating as quickly as possible. This is called the "Rule of the First Ten Minutes[9]" as the participation should be evident within the first ten minutes of any team building activity.

2. Does the activity enable people to think "outside" themselves?

Although this might sound like an esoteric principle, it is actually one of the most critical to consider.

Usually, people who attend team meetings are asking themselves some, if not all of the following questions:

• Why am I here? What value do I bring to the table?

9. This rule was developed and named by Practical Management Incorporated.

- I can't afford the time – I have emails piling up as we speak! Can I leave early?

- What truly is the purpose of this meeting?

If these questions are left to fester the result will be counter productive and team members will be unable to focus their full mental energies on the task at hand.

Therefore, a team building activity should get the participants focused as quickly as possible, so that individuals will not have the time or inclination to let their minds wander. Lack of focus will detract from their contribution to the process; and the business issue at hand will be severely compromised.

> **I would estimate that 90 percent of team builders, who fail to reach their original goals violate, at least partially, this business driven criterion.**

3. Is the activity business driven[10]?

This is the most critical aspect of any team building activity; and, is also the one most likely to be violated by a new Team Leader who has read too many "Games for Team Leaders" books!

If the participants cannot see the direct link from the activity they are engaged in to the business goal of the team, they will quickly turn-off and question the validity of the exercise.

Row, row, row your boat…

Again, this is not to say that we cannot have fun. This is also not to say that as Team Leaders we can't challenge people to think and work in new, "out-of-the-box" ways. However, it is crucial that, with any team activity, they see the business link as soon as possible.

---

10. This concept and name was developed and named by Practical Management Incorporated.

4. Is the activity perceived as safe?

Psychological safety is critical in the start-up phase of any team. If there is any chance that the activity will make any of the team members look foolish in front of their peers — avoid it.

I simply don't ascribe to the concept of individual embarrassment bringing a team closer together.

5. Is the activity efficient?

Simply put, is the time taken to conduct the team building activity appropriate for the length and the purpose of the meeting or initiative?

Again, the best activities are created as part of the team's day-to-day business activities. Having people (who normally don't work together) collaborating on a project, engaging team members in either decision-making or action planning, creating opportunities for the team to build consensus on an issue — *these are examples of the best team builders for any team.*

An astute Team Leader, who truly understands the concept of team building, will find that as the team progresses through its lifespan, *most team business activities will meet these five criteria without consciously designing them in that manner.*

TEAM BUILDING

The Five Critical Criteria

1. Does the activity enable participants to talk with each other?

2. Does the activity enable participants to think outside themselves?

3. Is the activity business-driven?

4. Is the activity perceived as safe?

5. Is the activity efficient?

The Facilitation Process

Assuming that you want to begin using a more facilitative approach with your team members on a regular basis, where do you start? What techniques do you use? How do you successfully implement them? The remainder of this chapter provides you with a practical, step-by-step process that will help you answer these and other important questions.

STEP 1: Selecting the appropriate discussion technique for facilitation skills

The Team Leader must first decide what type of discussion technique will be most effective in reaching her/his business goals. The process of facilitation ranges from leading tightly controlled discussions (Figure 2.3) to leading open interchange discussions (Figure 2.4).

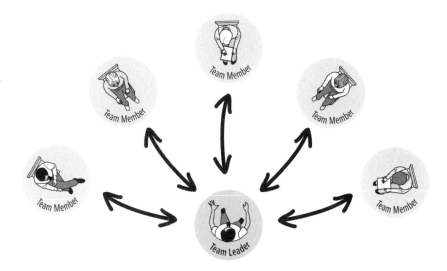

Figure 2.3 - Leading Tightly Controlled Discussions

When I teach facilitation skills to Team Leaders at our public and in-house seminars, I usually throw a ball out to the participants to illustrate the two different sets of dynamics. In Figure 2.3, the Team Leader tosses a ball out to an individual and then gets it back before it is tossed to another individual. This continues until most or all of the participants get a "turn." Tossing the ball is a metaphor for a Team Leader's questions and participant's subsequent answers — without allowing for individuals to comment on or question each other's replies.

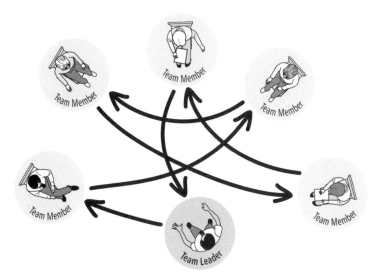

Figure 2.4 - Leading Open Interchange Discussions

Tightly controlled discussions are akin to brainstorming or list building, as they are more commonly known.

When you look at Figure 2.4, the Team Leader tosses the ball, in the form of a question or comment, which is then batted around amongst the team members in the form of agreements, disagreements, comments or elaborations. Once the discussion has fulfilled its purpose, the Team Leader takes control of the "ball" by either summarizing what has just transpired or by using it as a transition point to the next discussion.

Although the two approaches have many facilitation techniques in common *there is a definite difference in how each type of discussion is prepared for, facilitated and closed.*

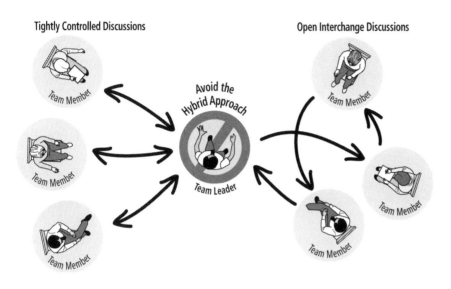

Tightly Controlled Discussions   Open Interchange Discussions

Figure 2.5 – Avoiding the Hybrid Approach

Avoiding the Hybrid Approach

As can be seen in Figure 2.5, many novice Team Leaders create their own problems by unknowingly facilitating a "hybrid" type of discussion. They subconsciously move back and forth between the two methods, resulting in confused, frustrated participants, and minimal movement toward the discussion's goal/s. For example, some participants will believe that they should be able to express their ideas without subsequent evaluation or discussion while other will believe their only role is to do exactly that – evaluate and discuss. Furthermore, if the Team Leader starts a tightly controlled discussion, i.e. list building or brainstorming, he/she can very easily get drawn into open discussions when people disagree and want to expand on ideas or discount others' ideas. In reality the Team Leader has gone from a tightly controlled discussion into an open interchange *without announcing any transition strategies to do so.*

Unless you are an experienced Team Leader with the requisite facilitation skills, my advice is that you do not attempt this hybrid approach; rather, select and stick with the method that will best help you reach your business goal.

However, if the Team Leader feels able to control the discussion, s/he very well might make a transition from a tightly controlled discussion to an open discussion. For example, if a team is discussing solutions that will enhance communication amongst four shifts in a 24-7 manufacturing operation, the Team Leader might engage the team in brainstorming (i.e. a tightly controlled discussion) a list of ideas, which would then be followed by an open discussion of each item. Looking at the pros and cons of each idea based on cost, time and resources via an open discussion and then agreeing upon a solution that fits would complete the discussion in this example.

In other words, it doesn't always have to be either or – however, one should start with one approach and then visibly move to another if doing so will aid in reaching the business goal.

Your most important consideration is to determine the intended business outcome of the discussion. I have consulted with many Team Leaders who plan to hold a weekly update meeting/discussion, for example, with only a very vague picture of what they are trying to achieve. In other words, they have not designed any systematic approach to reaching this non-existent outcome — and they then wonder why the team members perceive the meeting as a complete waste of time.

Some examples of what the purpose of a facilitative discussion might look like:

1. **The team will generate a workable list of ideas, problems or solutions to an issue.**

2. **The team will become more aware of a corporate policy.**

3. **The team will come to consensus on a specific action plan or implementation strategy.**

There are a myriad of outcomes, ranging from very specific decision making to awareness of issues that a Team Leader might choose to have the team discuss. *The key is for the Team Leader to know this prior to initiating the discussion, and then to determine the type of discussion that is best suited to the desired outcome.*

STEP 2 · When to Use List Building as a Discussion Technique

List building is not meant to be a complex tool for the analysis of ideas or concepts; rather, it is a way to expand a pool of ideas, solutions, possible causes or options.

The list building method of discussion method should be used:

✱ **When a large number of potential options, solutions, ideas, or methods are possible. If there are only two or three potential solutions to a problem, list building is not an appropriate discussion technique.**

✱ **For a relatively new team, that might be reticent about having too much open, frank or honest discussion. This type of discussion is a relatively easy method to get people engaged and involved quickly.**

When a team is trying to solve a problem or decide upon a course of action, it needs to develop a list of ideas from which to work. This could be a list of problems, a list of solutions, a list of options, a list of ideas etc. Therefore, the ability of the Team Leader to lead an effective list building or brain storming discussion (i.e. tightly controlled) is crucial.

How to Use List Building as a Discussion Technique

The following explanations outline the six rules for facilitating an effective list building/brain storming discussion.

RULE 1

Remember, vague questions will result in vague, unworkable answers.

Articulate a clear and concise question to the team.

Some thought has to be given beforehand to the question that you are going to pose to the team members – vague questions will result in vague responses that will prove to be useless.

Assume for a moment that a Team Leader wants input from his/her team on how to solve some team issues that center on the lack of communication between the day shift and the night shift. An example of a vague list-building question would be: "Let's come up with a list of ideas to help us solve our team problems." Answers to this question could range from communication issues to motivational issues, to workspace issues, to personality concerns, leadership concerns, financial concerns, parking space preference, and on and on.

A more specific question would be: "Lets come up with a list of ideas that will enhance team communication between the day shift team and the night shift team." While this question is more detailed and specific, you might still receive some of the same answers as you would from the first question. However, because the intent of the second question is clearly defined, the responses will be more specific and user-friendly.

RULE 2

Give people a minute or so to write down their responses prior to the list building discussion.

This is considered the "money" tip — it seems so obvious but very few Team Leaders use this technique; often they will either answer their own question, within a few seconds of asking it or call the participants by name to get an immediate response.

The academic argument for not writing ideas down first (in a brainstorming discussion) tends to center around wanting spontaneity of ideas so that the responses are quick and energizing for the group. You want team members to respond with the first thing that "pops into their head". Although speed is desirable (as will be detailed on p. 54), spontaneity is not lost by having people write down their responses first – *it is just delayed.*

The benefits of taking a minute or two so that the participants can first write down their responses to a specific question are three-fold:

1. **The act of committing answers to paper gives participants an opportunity to truly think about their answers, which results in higher quality responses.**

2. **For those who experience discomfort when participating in brainstorming sessions, the documentation of answers on paper provide them with a "hard copy" to read from if asked to vocalize and share their responses.**

3. **Giving team members a minute or two to write down their ideas, provides the Team Leader with some planning and analysis time before the actual discussion begins.**

Spontaneity does still occur and "spring boarding" of answers will result.

Provide a brief ground rule prior to beginning the tightly controlled discussion.

Once participants have had a few moments to jot down their ideas, the Team Leader needs to set a ground rule — *that no open discussion will take place at this point.* The need for rapid-fire answers with no comments, evaluations or elaboration must be emphasized. Human nature being the way it is, this ground rule will be violated, as people will feel the need to criticize, defend and question each other's responses. However, stating this rule at the outset, allows the Team Leader to gently remind the participants when the rule is violated, and that while no discussion is allowed at this point, there will be ample opportunity for open interchange during the ensuing discussion.

This ground rule lessens the chance of confrontation while allowing the Team Leader to maintain the pace and integrity of the list building session.

Create a sense of urgency.

Effective list building needs to be carried out at a moderate to quick pace. This is not to say that it needs to be carried out at the speed of light - each Team Leader's natural communication style and rhythm must be taken into consideration. However, as can be seen in Figure 2.6, whatever your speed and rhythm of communication naturally is, it needs to be taken "up a notch" during the list building process.

Creating a sense of urgency with the participants is beneficial because it reduces the likelihood of silence or "white space" between responses. If, during a list building discussion, the white space is too long — as little as three or four seconds – people have a tendency to do one of two things: they will either "fill the space" with discussion that is irrelevant or inappropriate or become so bored with the process that they embark on a "mental trip" to a tropical island. Either result will make it much more difficult for the Team Leader to keep the pace, flow and "spring boarding of ideas" that are crucial to a successful list building discussion.

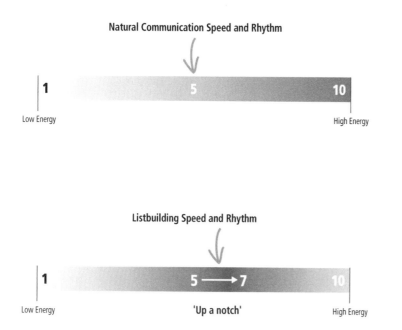

Natural Communication Speed and Rhythm

1   5   10

Low Energy   High Energy

Listbuilding Speed and Rhythm

1   5 ⟶ 7   10

Low Energy   'Up a notch'   High Energy

Figure 2.6 - Enhancing Your Pace During List building

There are a number of simple techniques that can be used to keep the group moving quickly through the brainstorming process.

> **Each of these basic techniques, when done in isolation from each other, seems fairly insignificant – however, in concert they become quite powerful.**

TECHNIQUE 1

Write quickly even if it results in a messy, unsightly sentence. If you are able to write both quickly and clearly then do it! Most Team Leaders have to sacrifice esthetics for speed - as long as you and the team can decipher the "chicken scratch" after the list building session, this is fine. Realize this is not a formal presentation or training program. If you were using flipcharts in those situations then neat and legible wording is appropriate. However, with list building the flipchart is akin to an artist's scratch pad. While the information is "hot" get it down — worry about deciphering it during the ensuing open interchange discussion.

TECHNIQUE 2

Use symbols and short forms and abbreviations for words or concepts wherever possible as this further minimizes "white space."

TECHNIQUE 3

Strike a forceful posture. Lean into the flip chart, marker poised – this sends a much different, yet subtle, message than leaning back on your heels, holding onto the flip chart and looking expectant and vague. A forceful stance is important, it shows the team that urgency is required and that, "We don't have all day to work on this."

TECHNIQUE 4

Constantly ask and prompt the group for more responses. Key words like "next", "another", "anymore?" "what else?" tend to motivate the team and maintain the pace. However, stay away from accolades, such as "great", "good job", "phenomenal", "good one" etc. Although such tributes might seem harmless, they can easily backfire on the Team Leader later in the discussion.

Assume for a moment that a Team Leader wants input from his/her team on how to solve some team issues that center on the lack of communication between the day shift and the night shift. During the list building discussion, a participant responds to your question about solutions that will enhance communication amongst four shifts in a 24-7 manufacturing operation— with, "Change to a wireless system," and you exclaim, "Great job" as you write it down quickly. Five minutes later, during the open interchange discussion, you and the team end up discounting and eliminating the "change to a wireless system" idea. The original respondent then says to him or herself, "The Team Leader just said it was a great idea, and now it has just been trashed, I don't get it?" The facilitation "purist" would respond to this situation by explaining that when the Team Leader originally said "Great job" it was a method of giving the participant positive feedback for the actual participation, not for the merits of the idea. However, in the heat of list building, when participants are not accustomed to a facilitative approach they might not be able to differentiate between the complimenting of their participation versus the quality of their actual idea. The result can be that they close down and become reluctant to further participate in the meeting.

Do not censor any responses during the list building discussion.

As soon as the Team Leader tells a participant that their idea won't work, e.g., "I'm sorry but we've tried that before" you have violated the core intent of the list building discussion. The participant now begins to wonder why you asked for his/her idea and might begin to believe that you are looking for a specific answer and POOF — the David Copperfield Illusion of Input has reared its ugly head[11]!

Remember, it is critical that all responses be given equal "airtime" — which is why they must be quickly written on the flipchart. The Team Leader should also be aware that other team members might

---

11. See Chapter 3 for a description of this Las Vegas phenomenon!

start to discount each other's responses during the list building process — at which point the Team Leader has to remind the group of the ground rule, set at the outset of the discussion, namely: to hold all comments until the ensuing open discussion. The Team Leader must quickly act on these team member comments as the peer group can close each other down faster than anyone, including the Team Leader.

RULE 6

Decide the most appropriate time to stop the list building discussion.

When the time comes to close down the list building discussion, there are some clear indicators – the most obvious being silence. However, if you feel that there are still more responses that could be drawn from the team, you might want to use the earlier concept of "white space" to your advantage. The question, "Are there any other angles that we have not pursued?" followed by a ten second pause and a inquisitive look, often will kick-start further discussion. Eventually, you will get to a point where the team is obviously "tapped out" and that it is time to stop the discussion.

The other indicator that it is time to close down the list building discussion is when you begin to get similar answers repeated but worded slightly differently. Therefore, as a Team Leader you need to be more than a blind scribe when writing down responses- keeping a mental note of what people are saying is crucial, that way you can spot the repetition when it starts.

QUICK REFERENCE CHECKLIST #2

Checklist for Effective List Building

✳ Have you articulated a clear and concise question?

✳ Have you given the team a few minutes to write down their responses prior to the actual discussion?

✳ Did you set the ground rule of "no open discussion" until the end of the list building?

✳ Did you create a "sense of urgency" during the actual discussion?

✳ Did you avoid censoring any responses?

✳ Did you close down the discussion at the appropriate juncture?

STEP 3 - What to do with the List and Making the Transition to an Open Interchange Discussion

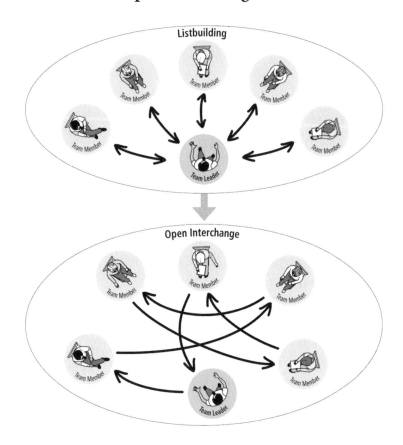

Figure 2.7A

Once you have created the list of options, solutions, ideas, methods, etc., you must decide what will be done with the list. In some cases you might want to thank the group for their contribution, take the list and make your own decisions based on its content.

This action is totally acceptable providing that you mentioned your intent to the team, beforehand.

If you do not mention this upfront, team tension will occur — as participants will naturally believe that if they created the list, they should be involved in prioritizing and, eventually, choosing the best options from the list.

Multi-Voting

When and if you choose to have the team involved in the prioritization and decision–making process, you will need a process to help you and the team work though the list. If you find that the list is fairly extensive (e.g. eight or more distinct, separate ideas) you might want to use a *Multi-Voting Process* — a method used to reduce the list to a workable number of items with a minimum expenditure of time and discussion and without creating the animosity that a "majority-rules" approach can spawn.

The procedure for multi-voting is as follows:

1. Briefly discuss each item with the specific purpose of ensuring that each is indeed a separate, distinct idea. Allowing duplications will dilute the voting process. Collectively, remove any duplication from the list.

2. Determine the number of votes for each team member. Generally, the number of votes is equal to one-third of the ideas on the list. If for example there are nine ideas that are on the brainstormed list, each team member will have three votes. They must vote on three different ideas that they believe, based on their experience, are the best answers.

3. Number each item on the list. Ask each person to select and write down the items for which s/he will vote.

4. Conduct the vote, placing totals beside the ideas on the flipchart. Generally, voting is done by a show of hands although if there is a need for confidentiality, team members can write down their votes and give them to the Team Leader.

5. Reduce the list by eliminating those items with either no votes or with relatively few votes. Usually, there will be a "breaking point" between the lower and higher vote "getters". In the following example there is a natural break between the options that received eight votes and the options that received seven votes and the rest of the items that received five or less. In this case you would first choose to examine the higher vote options before eliminating or examining the items that had five votes or less (see Figure 2.7).

Figure 2.7 Multi Vote Example

6. It is important that even if there appears to be a "clear winner" the vote should not make the final decision for the team. The purpose of the multi-voting process is to reduce a potentially unmanageable list of items to a reasonable number of items that will then be discussed in detail through the open interchange approach. In most cases, this reduction will yield anywhere from two to four items for detailed open discussion.

7. If, after the first multi-voting session, you still have numerous items with a high number of votes, then renumber those items and repeat the multi-voting process until the items are pared down to a manageable number for open discussion. For example, if you had eight items with six or more votes each, you would renumber each item from one to eight, give everyone three votes (i.e. the one-third rule) and do another show of hands. In the majority of situations, two rounds of multi-voting will be sufficient to reduce the list to a manageable number.

Conversely, if the number of items is relatively few (i.e. less than eight) you might decide that an open exploration of each item might be necessary to determine which will be adopted.

At either of these stages it would now be appropriate to lead an open interchange discussion, see Step 4.

STEP 4 - When to Use an Open Interchange Discussion

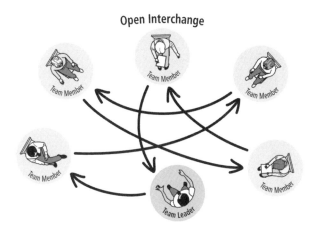

Open discussions are a method for determining which option, idea, solution, etc. would be most appropriate to consider or implement in a business situation.

The open discussion method should be used:

* **When a small number of potential options, solutions, ideas or methods are being considered.**

* **If there are numerous potential solutions to a problem, list building and multi-voting should occur prior to the actual open discussion.**

* **When a strong consensus is needed, it is critical to have an honest, open discussion so that all team members can air their concerns and hear each other's points of view.**

How to Conduct an Open Interchange Discussion

The pace and dynamics of an open interchange discussion are markedly different from those of a tightly controlled discussion, therefore, the techniques for effective facilitation must be altered accordingly. When leading open interchange discussions, there are many challenges— some of the most prevalent being:

* **The team taking the discussion off topic**

* **Side conversations breaking out between members**

* **Team members being overly negative, resulting in the rest of the team becoming demotivated**

* **Obstinate arguers getting their own way**

Therefore, to help meet these challenges, Team Leaders need to develop skills in three critical areas:

The Three Techniques

A. Involvement and Questioning Techniques

The gift of involving team members in focused, productive discussions is primarily based on one critical skill set – the ability, at a moment's notice, to construct and ask different types of participative, thought-provoking questions.

B. Choreography Techniques[12]

Understanding how your position and movement in front of the team impacts the dynamics of a discussion is critical in both preventing and dealing with disruptions to the process.

C. Control Methods

Closing down disruptive behaviour in a respectful, assertive manner as opposed to closing out the participant in an aggressive, disrespectful manner is an "art-form" that involves both strategy and diplomacy.

A - Involvement and Questioning Techniques

The single most important tool a Team Leader has available — for leading participative, team-oriented open-interchange discussions

12. This concept and name was developed and named by Practical Management Incorporated.

— is the question. Learning to ask questions, many times "on-the-fly" and being comfortable doing so, requires a good deal of practice along with some fundamental techniques. Although there are literally dozens of different ways to ask a question, my experience has shown that *if you can master the following five techniques, then a productive, participative discussion should result.*

When asking questions, many Team Leaders make the mistake of not allowing team members enough time to answer the question. In order to respond, team members need time to do what you want them to do – think! This is often difficult to do because it often produces… THE BIG SILENCE – a condition that can be deadly for both team members and the Team Leader. Although a few seconds of silence is necessary for team members to mentally process and then offer an answer, repeated and elongated silence is both de-motivating and embarrassing for all concerned. Therefore, in order to overcome the "big silence" and create focused, open discussion the following techniques are required.

EXAMPLE
The Team Leader and team discussing a list of communication ideas in the 24-7 manufacturing operation (from our earlier list building discussion) is the example used to illustrate how these questions can be specifically used.

1. Ask the same question twice... but vary the way you ask it.

In an open discussion, you might need to ask the same question twice, in order to stimulate both thinking and a response. By varying the way you ask the question — the second time around— you create another perspective that will help team members to assimilate their thoughts, and respond appropriately.

"Looking at the first item on the list, how would we actually conduct a communication assessment on the shop floor? (Pause) If I want someone to conduct a communication assessment, how would they go about doing it?"

2. First, find out who has experience with the proposed idea; then, ask your question.

If you do not know the extent and degree of team members' experience with the topic under discussion, this technique is, by far, the most effective approach for getting members involved.

"How many of you have been involved in a communication assessment process? (Show of hands – Matt and others put up their hands!) "From your experience, Matt, what are some of the most common problems when doing this?"

3. Get more team members involved by using a deflection or ricochet question in response to another team members direct question or statement.

Although technically speaking this is a way to respond to questions rather than a question asking technique, it deserves mention here.

The deflection question addresses a team member's specific question or statement by deflecting it out to the group to comment on — before you say anything. You might still choose to respond, but only after you have heard the replies to your deflected question. The following example helps to illustrate this simple, yet powerful technique:

Employee Lauren to Team Leader Blake: "What do you think we should do about the quality issue?"

Team Leader Blake (using a deflection question): "Before I comment Lauren, what are some other perspectives from the rest of the team?"

Employee Tom: "Personally I believe we need to conduct a quality audit before we can determine the root cause of the current quality issue."

> **Team Leader Blake:** " I would tend to agree with Tom and we also might want to bring in some outside expertise to help us conduct that audit."

Note that Team Leader Blake is careful to acknowledge Tom's contribution while still adding some value to Tom's comment. Tom answers Lauren's question due to the facilitation skills of the Team Leader Blake.

The ricochet question addresses a team member's question or statement by directing it to someone who they know has specific experience with the topic under discussion, to comment on first. Again the Team Leader might choose to respond, but only after s/he has heard the responses from the team initiated by the deflected question. The following scenario adapted from the previous one, helps to illustrate this technique:

> **Employee Lauren to Team Leader Blake:** "What do you think we should do about the quality issue?"

> **Team Leader Blake (using a ricochet question):** "Before I comment Lauren, Tom you have had some experience with this, what are your thoughts?"

> **Employee Tom:** "Personally I believe we need to conduct a quality audit before we can determine the root cause of the current quality issue."

> **Team Leader Blake:** " I would tend to agree with Tom and we also might want to bring in some outside expertise to help us conduct that audit."

4. Use team members' backgrounds or experience as a way of inviting them into the discussion.

This technique assumes that you are well aware of the individual and collective experience that the team brings to the table. As questions are meant to be discussion devices and not oral exams, the way you phrase the segue to the question is vital — especially if people are to participate voluntarily. By using question "intros" such as "Based on your years of experience…" "From what you've seen before…" "Bill, you have had 20 years in the business — what do you think?" team members actually want to participate as you are actually "patting them on the back" prior to asking the question.

5. During real-life scenarios and questions (either indirect or direct), use team members' names to help maintain their interest and enhance participation levels.

Addressing team members by name is the most effective way to keep them mentally engaged and avoid the "tropical vacation" syndrome — discussed earlier. Furthermore, if names are used in a relevant scenario it enhances the chances of people responding in a meaningful manner.

This can be done either indirectly:

"Let's talk about the enhanced voice mail system idea. Assume Bill is the supervisor of the day shift and Doug is the supervisor of the night shift. How would an enhanced voice mail system increase the communication between the two of them?"

Or directly:

"Let's talk about the enhanced voice mail system idea. Bill, you are the supervisor of the day shift and Doug, the supervisor of the night shift. So my question is to either of you - how would an enhanced voice mail system increase the communication between the two of you?"

If you can master these five question-asking techniques, you are well on the way to competently leading focused and participatory team discussions. Furthermore, *by following the three tips below* you will prevent many of the disruptions that plague the novice discussion leader.

TIP 1 - Avoid calling or depending on a few reliable, vocal members.

If you rely on them, so will the rest of the team resulting in very little participation. Direct questions away from those team members and make direct eye contact with those from whom you want responses.

TIP 2 - Be conversational in your approach to asking questions - as you would during any discussion in which you're really interested in the answer.

Listen carefully and with your full attention. Respond to the team members' answers in a way that indicates you heard precisely what they said. The best way to do so is to ask another question based on the team members' responses or use their words in your response to their answers.

TIP 3 - Go out of your way to make sure your questions are clearly stated.

The most common reason why you might get little response to your questions is because the team can't decipher what you want. Learn to add transitions or cues to your questions, e.g. rather than blurting out, "Why are open-ended questions important?", preface the

question with "In a team discussion in which you want full participation…". Or rather than, "Why is it important to improve communication?" try, "Given that our shift communication has not
been very effective lately…"

B – Choreography

The choreography (position and movement in front of a team) of a
facilitated discussion or meeting *is a critical but rarely discussed
method* of enhancing involvement and preventing disruptive
behaviour. A Team Leader's physical presence and how he or she
uses it can greatly affect the dynamics of a discussion with a team.

There are three rules of choreography.

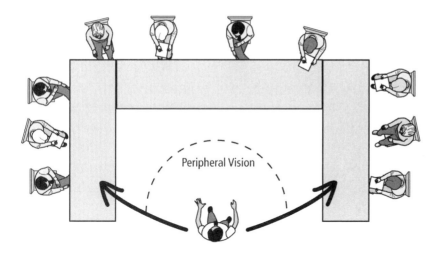

Peripheral Vision

Figure 2.8 Filling one's peripheral vision

RULE 1 Always keep the entire group within your peripheral vision and keep your peripheral vision full.

Unless everyone is kept within the Team Leader's peripheral vision
(Figure 2.8), the participants will quickly engage in side discussions,

or become disinterested, because they feel ignored. Conversely, when you are too close to the team members (Figure 2.9), you invade their comfort zone, thereby causing them to become either tentative or overly aggressive - neither result is desirable.

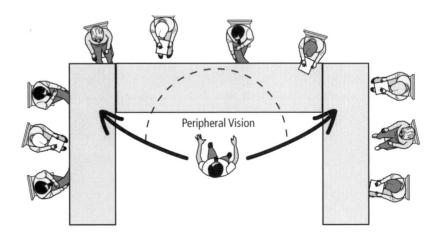

Figure 2.9 Standing too close

When the Team Leader is located back, far from the tables (Figure 2.10) his/her peripheral vision is not full; and this position creates a feeling of distance from the team and a sense of a one-way lecture rather than an open, participatory discussion.

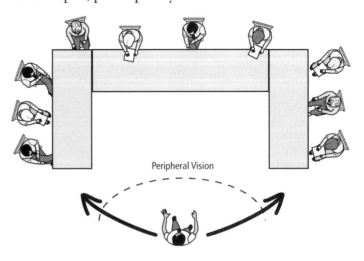

Figure 2.10 Standing too far away

Spending the majority of your time at the "Team Leader" position in Figure 2.8 allows everyone a comfort level with your positioning — and keeps people engaged, through the use of your eyes and body position.

RULE 2 Always keep a distance between you and the person/s with whom you are talking.

When you are having a one-on-one discussion for a few moments with one person in the team you still want the rest of the team actively listening. Therefore, *if you walk further away* from that individual (Figure 2.11), you abide by Rule One as well as forcing both you and the other person to speak louder. Although this goes against natural courtesy, it does allows you to carry on the conversation with the individual while, simultaneously, keeping the entire team engaged — through both occasional eye contact, as well as your open body positioning at the front of the meeting room.

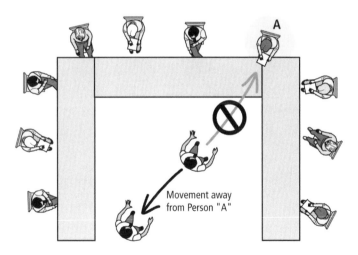

Movement away
from Person "A"

Figure 2.11 Moving away

RULE 3. Set-up the room to promote open discussion

In a perfect world, Team Leaders would use the wide "U" shape as illustrated in the previous figures. The first two rules of choreography are more efficiently applied with this type of room set-up, which avoids "dashing down the runway" (Figure 2.12).

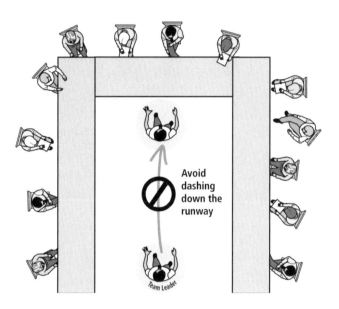

Figure 2.12 Avoid dashing down the runaway

However, in many instances, the Team Leader must try to follow these guidelines while dealing with a more traditional, rectangular or boardroom style table set-up. Notice in Figure 2.13 the flip chart and Team Leader are positioned at the side of the table versus the end of the table. Circumstances might dictate that this is not possible, especially if the room is too small or the A.V. equipment is bolted to the floor at the end of the table. However, if you can make the transition to the side, chances are you will notice a distinct difference in the team dynamics.

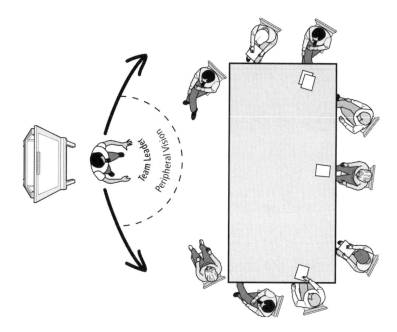

Figure 2.13 Choreography and the board room table

The position at the end of the table has a long history of power that is still alive in many of today's corporate boardrooms. Although participation can still occur in this set-up, it usually is limited to a very formal, almost parliamentary process. For most discussions, where team participation is critical, you want to effectively neutralize that power position. If you set-up on the side of the table, and move back slightly, thereby enhancing your peripheral vision, a similar "feel" to the wide "U" set-up will result.

C – Control Methods

Closing down disruptive behaviour in a respectful, assertive manner as opposed to closing out the participant in an aggressive, disrespectful manner is an "art-form" that involves both strategy and diplomacy. For example, a Team Leader can easily close down the team during an open discussion if they exhibit any of the following behaviour:

✳ **They get argumentative with the participants**

✳ **They are sarcastic to the team**

✳ **They quickly discount team members' ideas**

The challenge, with closing down inappropriate behaviour, is to keep the rest of the team on board. In other words, if one team member feels slighted, it can create a ripple effect amongst the other members, as they start to think, "If the Team Leader treats Bob that way when he answers a question, I am not going to put myself in front of that firing line!" By closing one person down, you might effectively close down the entire team.

When the slighted team member is aggressive and barks back at the Team Leader, this can open up the floodgates for antagonistic behaviour by the rest of the team, resulting in an ineffective, stressful meeting.

Figure 2.14 outlines five of the most typical types of behaviour that a Team Leader will encounter during an open discussion; the subtle approaches to dealing with such behaviour; and a more overt approach. However, it is critical that a Team Leader does not confuse an overt approach with being loud and obnoxious — overt is meant to be more assertive and obvious *while still maintaining the respect and self-esteem of the team member involved.*

Figure 2.14 Dealing with Disruptive Behaviour

When the team members:	Subtle Approaches	Overt Approaches
1. Engage in prolonged side conversations.	a. Move toward the "side conversationalists" while still leading a discussion with the rest of the team – your physical presence will quickly close down the side conversation. b. Use their names in a scenario question – hearing one's name usually will stop the side conversation.	a. Go silent – their conversation will become much more evident. b. Politely interrupt with "Folks- one conversation at a time please."
2. Argue for the sake of arguing (Usually done as a result of frustration with the Team Leader, the team, a process or the company).	a. Acknowledge their concerns and ask for a solution or an option to their issue. b. Ask the other team members what their perspective is on the issue. Note: There is risk to this approach as the team might agree with the "arguer."	a. Acknowledge their concerns and restate the importance of sticking with the agenda and its timelines. b. Acknowledge their concerns and suggest they be taken "off-line."
3. Are always the first ones to answer a question (effectively closing down the other team members).	a. You state "Lots of great answers from this side of the room – how about some from the other side." b. You state "Thanks Bill for the answer. Let me get another from someone else."	a. You state "Bob – hang on a second. Let me get a response from someone else." b. Chat off-line to the individual acknowledging their contribution but emphasizing the importance of participation by everyone.
4. Use electronic devices (i.e. cell phone, laptops, pagers, etc.) thereby distracting the rest of the team.	a. Set out a "ground rule" upfront minimizing or eliminating electronic devices.	a. Politely ask people to turn off devices so that everyone can focus their attention on the discussion at hand.
5. Do not take the discussion seriously and become jokers or "hecklers".	a. Re-emphasize to the entire group the importance of the discussion at hand.	a. Politely ask "hecklers" to focus their energy on the discussion at hand.

QUICK REFERENCE CHECKLIST #3

Checklist for Leading Effective Open Interchange Discussions

* Have you considered what the desired outcome for the open discussion is? Is it a decision, an action plan and/or a problem being solved?

* Have you considered whether the open discussion is the result of a transition from a tightly controlled discussion or is it a "stand-alone" method of discussion?

* Have you planned a few open-ended questions to pose to the team at various intervals throughout the open discussion to get team members talking?

* Have you set-up the meeting room so that it is conducive to open, honest discussions?

* Have you reviewed the various control methods so that you can effectively close disruptive team members down without closing them out?

* Have you considered what the next steps are once the team has made the decision or solved the problem?

Summary

This chapter outlined and explained the types of discussion skills (i.e. facilitation skills) that a Team Leader must possess in order to run a participatory, open and productive discussion with their work team. Hopefully, you will now understand that the skill of facilitation is more than a simple skill that requires a flip chart, a toxic-smelling marker, and the ability to proclaim, "Lets discuss things."

If you can master the list building and open discussion techniques and avoid some of the pitfalls of the team building process, your competence in leading productive and focused discussions will be greatly enhanced. As with any solid team leadership principle or practice, a plan must be established before starting the discussion, *competent facilitation happens by design – not default.*

3 Repairing Your Team
When Things Go Wrong

Even the most dedicated, well-intentioned and competent Team Leader will, at some time, face the daunting challenge of examining a team that is currently not reaching its objectives and then deciding on a course of action to remedy the situation. Here, I outline the activities and strategies required to rebuild a team based on some of the most common root causes I have observed during the past twenty years.

This chapter examines some of the most common reasons that teams run into trouble, and then details the micro-level skills and strategies required by the Team Leader to get the team back on track.

As a Team Leader, how does one go about "repairing" a team that has lost its drive or focus? Theories and activities abound, ranging from outdoor activities to simulated team problem-solving exercises to weekend retreats. Although all of these initiatives have some merit, *the most effective way to re-build a team is for a Team Leader and the team to focus on their day-to-day behaviour as opposed to engaging in an annual or bi-annual "event".*

Interpersonal behaviour, such as active listening skills, conflict resolution skills, motivational techniques, and appropriate communication skills are crucial for both the team and its leader on a daily basis — *however without the strategies to apply them, the skill sets are ineffective.*

Before We Begin… the Myth of a Team Leader as Neutral Facilitator

One of the most common problems I observe with new Team Leaders is that they have come to believe they can act like, what is commonly referred to as, a neutral facilitator. *This is a myth.* A Team Leader can act as a facilitator with his/her work group and lead a very productive, interactive meeting using various facilitation and discussion techniques. However, *the term neutral —when used in conjunction with facilitation strategies — implies that there is no vested interest in the outcome.*

A Team Leader is accountable for what goes on with his/her work team, therefore, the nature of organizational hierarchy dictates that the Team Leader must have a vested interest in the outcome of any business discussion and therefore can not be neutral in the true sense.

Many a Team Leader, having just read the latest article professing the effectiveness of neutral facilitation, has tried to play such a role while facilitating problem solving, strategic or business planning with his or her team and, consequently, run into disastrous results.

For example, I was personally involved in a situation where a team of colleagues (all Team Leaders) and myself were invited to a day long, offsite meeting being facilitated by our vice-president (i.e. our boss). At the beginning, he stated he would be our "facilitator" for the day and that he would use the experience of the eight people in the room to determine a new location for one of our regional offices. He claimed that we were the experts and that wherever we decided the new office should be relocated, he would commit to the decision and take it forward to his boss, the president.

On the surface, this sounded as though we were to have the opportunity to contribute to a critical organizational decision that, traditionally, would be made by a more senior level manager — very motivating to say the least!

However, it soon became apparent that every time we, as a team, came up with an idea with which the VP disagreed with, he very masterfully, through his expert facilitation skills, dismissed our input. And, he did it in such a way that at first we did not recognize his tactics. Eventually one of the sharper wits on our team audibly muttered, "Why don't you just tell us what location you want for the new office so we can stop wasting our time and get some actual work done?!"

Once the uncomfortable silence was broken the VP sheepishly replied, "Well, I was hoping that we could relocate our office to the intersection of XYZ as that seems to be an area of high growth and customer traffic."

The impact of this situation can be viewed in Figure 3.1.

The David Copperfield Illusion of Input

In any team environment it takes time to build trust, not only between individual team members, but also between team members and the Team Leader. Day to day activities will either help or hinder the process — activities such as daily communications, the clarification of expectations, motivating work, active encouragement, facing challenges, etc. If, most of the time, the Team Leader does the 'right stuff', trust levels will gradually build. However, when team members are made to believe that they have input into a major decision and then find out that they were victims of the David Copperfield Illusion of Input (coined at our training sessions in Las Vegas!) their level of trust in their Team Leader

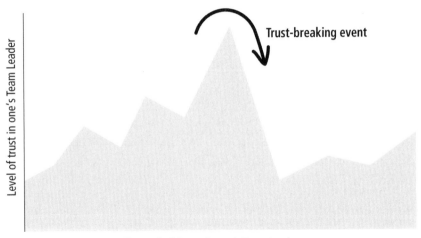

Figure 3.1 - The Building and Breaking of Team Trust

immediately and dramatically declines (Figure 3.1). While Team members tend to trust again, it will take much longer for them to reach similar levels of trust — assuming that they ever do.

Our VP in this vignette, whether consciously or subconsciously, attempted to be a neutral facilitator (namely, having no vested interest) in a decision that he was ultimately accountable for and in which he had a strong vested interest.

This is not to say that Team Leaders cannot have strong discussion (hence facilitation) skills and be very effective in their application. However, the previous vignette illustrates that *a Team Leader cannot be neutral when it comes to facilitating work teams that report to him/her directly.*

The Four Most Common Team Problems and How to Repair Them

	SYMPTOM	POSSIBLE CAUSE	SOLUTION
	1. Inappropriate behaviour and lack of focus on what is important .	No clear ground rules or code of conduct either created or enforced.	Creation and/or reiteration of ground rules.
	2. Disinterested, apathetic, confused team members.	Absence of clear, mutually understood roles and goals.	Assertive discussion and clarification of team and individual goals and roles.
	3. When team consensus decision-making opportunities arise there is arguing, distrust and confusion resulting eventually in a "who cares" attitude.	Not truly understanding what consensus decision-making involves.	Discussion of what consensus decision-making is and how to achieve it.
	4. Inappropriate or inadequate communication amongst team members and/or Team Leader.	Team members do not understand the why's and how's behind inter-team communications.	Discussion of the appropriate type of communication media and strategies when and how to use them.

Figure 3.2 Team Symptoms, Possible Causes and Solutions

PROBLEM #1

	SYMPTOM	POSSIBLE CAUSE	SOLUTION
	1. Inappropriate behaviour and lack of focus on what is important.	No clear ground rules or code of conduct either created or enforced.	Creation and/or reiteration of ground rules.

Figure 3.2 outlines some of the most common problems and symptoms that face a team, followed by a brief description of the solutions. A more detailed description of each of the problems and solutions follows.

Now, let's expand on this chart with an outline of specific actions you can take to remedy these problems.

Creation or Reiteration of Ground Rules

The concept of creating a set of ground rules or behavioural operating principles for a team is not new. *Ground rules are critical in helping keep the team on track in terms of what is acceptable and non-acceptable behaviour.* Although some might consider ground rules to be unnecessary or even demeaning, they provide Team Leaders with a behavioural template that they can refer back to when team members lose focus.

When ground rules are set, team members know what is expected of them, especially in a team-meeting environment. Although setting ground rules will not necessarily eliminate all inappropriate behaviour, it makes everyone that much more aware of what is appropriate and what is not. In addition, ground rules allow the Team Leader to more effectively deal with inappropriate behaviour when it arises. For example, if Bob continually cuts off Sue in mid-sentence, during a team discussion, the Team Leader can gently remind Bob that he needs to respect Ground Rule 4 which states, "All team members can articulate their opinions, uninterrupted."

Furthermore, as teams mature, not only will the Team Leader "call" team members on their behaviour, so will fellow team members — *resulting in more focused, less confrontational team meetings and discussions.*

Listed on the following pages are two examples of some common ground rules that teams create. By no means is this a "must have" or exclusive list. Each team will create their own ground rules based on their specific environment and culture. Also note that although the two examples are most appropriate to formal team meetings, *they can be easily adapted to become a behavioural template for day-to-day team interactions.*

GROUND RULES - Example 1

1. Do not interrupt during discussions.
2. If disagree, explain why.
3. Everyone listens and participates; seeks understanding.
4. Critique process and progress; attack ideas, not people.
5. Make decisions by consensus.
6. No substitutes.
7. If you miss a meeting, it is your responsibility to get updated before the next one.
8. Distribute the minutes to team members only.
9. Quorum is five members in five minutes after starting time. If five members are not present, the meeting will be cancelled.
10. No visitors without invitation.
11. Minutes should be distributed as soon as possible after meeting, but no later than two days before the next meeting.

GROUND RULES - Example 2

1. Demonstrate appropriate professional behaviour at all times.

2. A quorum will be two thirds of team membership.

3. Meetings will start on time if a quorum is present. If a quorum is not present within five minutes after starting time, the meeting will be cancelled.

4. An agenda is required for each meeting:
   - agenda might be modified at beginning of each meeting.
   - time limits for each agenda item will be set.
   - next meeting agenda will be determined at end of each meeting.

5. If time limit on a topic is reached, the team will determine whether to continue the discussion and adjust the agenda or continue the topic at the next meeting.

6. No meeting interruptions.

7. Ideas are to be freely exchanged - everyone is equal.

8. Team decisions are to be made by consensus.

A Word of Caution

If you decide that setting ground rules is vital to getting your team back on track, ensure that you initiate the process but allow the team to generate the actual list. It is easy to fall into the trap of creating the list yourself, presenting it to the team and then asking for their acceptance. If you follow this course, you are likely to get puzzled looks, a few grunts of approval, some nods and then people will move on to the business at hand paying absolutely no attention to the newly created ground rules. One of the prime benefits of ground rules is not only the creation of a code of conduct, but also the ownership that is created though the act of discussing and agreeing upon ground rules. However, with a severely dysfunctional team, the Team Leader might have to take a more active role and create the majority of the ground rules since the team might not possess the appropriate state of mind or collective competencies to discuss and then agree upon them.

> **Team members will be that much more motivated to adhere to the rules if they created them.**

PROBLEM #2

	SYMPTOM	POSSIBLE CAUSE	SOLUTION
	2. Disinterested, apathetic, confused team members.	Absence of clear, mutually understood roles and goals.	Assertive discussion and clarification of team and individual goals and roles.

Discussion of the Specific Roles of Team Members and Their Corresponding Goals

As teams evolve, so do the goals for which Team Leaders are accountable. Although any competent Team Leader understands that goal setting is an integral part of the leadership process, it is even more crucial when team members seem disinterested or apathetic. Assuming that the apathetic behaviour is not caused by factors outside the workplace or because of a poor fit between the team

> A meeting that helps to clarify the goals and, where possible, solicits the team members' input into action plans that support the goals, can go a long way to alleviate their disinterest.

member and their specific job function, goal clarification might be necessary.

Furthermore, a team member's role tends to evolve with time, especially when re-orgs, downsizing or mergers are thrown into the mix. A Customer Service Representative (CSR) on an IT Help Desk team might be originally hired to listen to a customer's problem, troubleshoot and then help the customer fix the problem themselves via phone or online. Over time, due to increasingly complex technology problems or greater service expectations from the client, it might become necessary to actually visit the client on site and fix the problem in conjunction with the client. Although this would seem a natural evolution of the role, various parameters around this role will change dramatically: e.g. number of calls taken per day vs. on-site visits, the tools and technology required to solve more complex, offsite problems, etc. *Role clarification on a regular basis is necessary in any progressive team.*

My experience has shown that a team member's goals and roles are interwoven and that even the most motivated team member will become confused, apathetic and/or disinterested if the Team Leader doesn't help redefine the goals and roles on a continual basis.

Therefore, goal and role clarification by the Team Leader should include the following four elements:

1. Help the team members experience – physically, mentally or emotionally – why they need to perform in a certain manner.

Disinterested team members often lose sight of why they are to perform in a certain manner to a specific level – this is especially prevalent after a merger, downsizing or re-organization. However, even without a major organizational shake-up, team members can lose sight of their goals and the purpose behind them.

It is one thing to explain to a team member the importance of the goals and how they fit together within the organization. It is another thing *if you as the Team Leader can devise a method for them to experience the 'why' or importance of the goal.*

A few years ago, I had the experience of working with a medium-sized manufacturer that was plagued by quality problems. The Team Leader would try everything in his power to have the front line team members be more attentive to the detail required to manufacture high quality, tight tolerance, car door trim. Rewards, punitive action, bribery and downright verbal abuse were all used unsuccessfully. Although he had some success by holding a meeting with some of the key team members — to concisely explain the importance of high quality to both the team and the department itself (i.e., poor quality = being fired as the vendor = poor reputation = potential loss of contracts = closing their doors = unemployed team members) — for the most part, quality did not significantly improve.

It wasn't until the Team Leader bussed the majority of workers 50 kms to their customer's plant — where their door trim was being inserted on the actual completed automobile—that he finally had some success. By letting his team members see how their trim was applied to the finished exterior of the automobile and how as much as 30 percent of the trim was being tossed angrily into huge trash cans because it didn't fit correctly, it became painfully obvious why the quality and tolerances were so important.

While this experience alone did not solve all of their quality problems, there was a dramatic attitude adjustment — once the team members experienced the "why" behind their goals.

> The experience of watching their hard work literally get 'trashed' seemed to tug at some intrinsic motivation around the team's "pride of work."

2. Help create links between individual, team, department and organizational goals.

Apathy and/or disinterest are by-products of the confusion that arises when team members are uncertain as to how their individual goals tie directly into the team goals, then into the departmental/divisional goals which in turn lead into the overall organizational business goals. (See Figure 3.3)

If a front-line customer service team member is told that when s/he troubleshoots a customer's software problem over the phone, the call must be completed within three minutes — that might be a very realistic expectation. However, if that team member has no idea of how this fits into the team goal of reducing current wait times by 15 percent, the department will not reach its customer service metrics of at least 95 percent satisfied customers, which, in turn, will violate the organization's goal of providing the most timely service for their specific market segment—then as a Team Leader, you have a problem.

Furthermore, if team member Dave, sees Sarah, a fellow team member, spending five to ten minutes per call, he might view this as inequitable. However, if Dave had been informed that Sarah, as the most competent and experienced team member, specifically looks after the customer calls that involve both software and a hardware problem (i.e. a different role), he might be more understanding and hence motivated.

The Team Leader should make assertive efforts to explain the varied contributions that each team member makes, and should make the links for those team members who cannot make the connections for themselves.

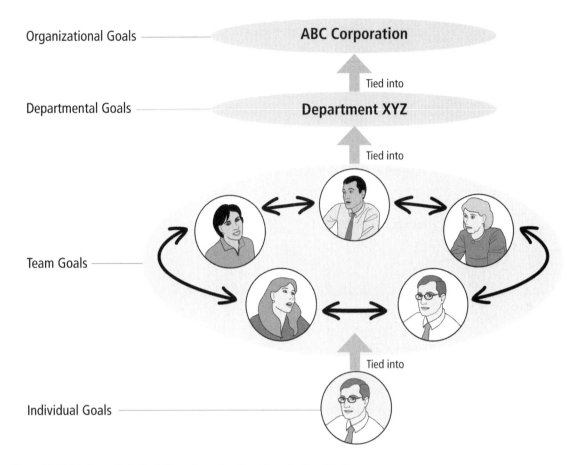

Figure 3.3 Link Between Individual, Team, Department and Organizational Goals

3. Articulate goals that are Measurable, Achievable, Realistic, and Controllable (M.A.R.C.).

Although the science of how to set an accurate business goal is not new, its importance has not diminished over time. On a frequent basis, it is not uncommon to hear team members complain that they are unclear on exactly what they are to do as part of their job function. Although such confusion might seem unfathomable to some of the more experienced Team Leaders reading this, there is no doubt that with the speed of technology, global competition and strides in innovation, the need for organizations to constantly readjust organizational goals has never been more pronounced. Executives might be very clear on the organization's new direction, but unless this is communicated downwards —in a clear, concise and frequent manner through to the Team Leader who can then turn this information into performance goals and objectives — it is extremely confusing to the front-line team members.

> **To achieve a team that is truly high performance, goals must be an intrinsic part of the performance management system and must be Measurable, Achievable, Realistic and Controllable (M.A.R.C.).**

For example, Dave, the Customer Service team member we mentioned earlier received one of his performance goals that reads:

> **Provide solutions to a minimum of three customers per hour with a satisfaction rating of 95 percent as measured by the Customer Quality Index.**

The fact that the goal is quantifiable makes it *measurable.* As other team members with similar skill sets and experience can and have met these goals, we can safely say that the goal is *both achievable and realistic.* Finally, as it is something that Dave has the skill set to do, and the infrastructure surrounding him is sound (e.g., phone access, troubleshooting manuals, the ability to elevate the problem if required) then, assuming there are no natural disasters; it is a very *controllable goal.*

Again, as roles evolve so do goals — a goal that meets the M.A.R.C. rule today might not meet the M.A.R.C. rule in the next two months. Furthermore, in a start up division, goals might have to be created without any template from past experience — therefore time, patience and ongoing dialogue and coaching will be crucial to hone in and fine-tune the goal-setting process.

4. Outline tangible evidence that the goals have been met and provide appropriate coaching if they have not.

Again the example used previously is quite explicit in terms of what the expectations of Dave, the Customer Service Rep are.

Provide solutions to a minimum of three customers per hour with a satisfaction rating of 95 percent as measured by the Customer Quality Index.

When the time comes to actually measure whether Dave has met this goal, obviously there are other factors that have to be considered, such as learning curve time, amount of Team Leader coaching required, Dave's ability to interact and influence other team members around him when he needs their expertise, etc.

The bottom line is that providing Dave's Team Leader spends the time up front, in determining what are measurable, achievable, controllable and realistic goals and reviews them regularly as Dave's role evolves, the measurement of performance should be a straightforward process. However, if Dave is having difficulty in meeting his goals, then he will need on-going coaching from his Team Leader.

Coaching to Meet Performance Goals

This part of this book could be another book itself — therefore the goal of this section is to outline a simple but effective coaching model that a Team Leader can use to help his or her team members meet their critical performance goals. Even a Project Leader whose team members do not directly report to him/her will find this five–step process[13] easy to implement.

Assume that Dave has been in his new role for a few months now, and it is obvious that he is struggling with one of his performance goals. The coaching process that his Team Leader should follow is:

1. Specify the aspects of performance that need improvement

Be specific and concise (e.g. solving only two customer issues per hour rather than three).

13. Adapted from the Development Dimensions International (DDI) coaching model.

Maintain self-esteem by mentioning related aspects that are positive (e.g. Dave's follow up documentation and closing of the file is carried out competently).

2. Indicate why his inability to meet the new role is of concern

Outline the specific effect on the team, department and other stakeholders if necessary (e.g. creates additional work for other team members and influences budgetary considerations for next fiscal year).

3. Ask for Dave's perspective and rationale

Avoid impulsive judgment (i.e. avoid blaming as Dave explains why he feels the task is too difficult).

Clarify facts and probe further (e.g. if Dave complains there is not enough time to effectively work with three clients an hour, probe deeper into what solutions he is providing and his current management of priorities and time).

4. Discuss specific actions that will improve performance and how they must be implemented

Allow the team member an opportunity to determine what needs to be done to meet his or her goals (i.e. ask Dave, what specific strategies must be employed to meet his goals).

If unable to devise a strategy, then "'paint a clear picture" of what must be done to meet performance expectations (i.e. if Dave cannot come up with a solution then the Team Leader must lay out a specific set of actions).

5. Discuss and agree upon when actions must be taken and appropriate follow-up date/s

Set up time for specific follow-up (e.g. a meeting next Monday to jointly discuss Dave's progress and strategies that have worked well and not so well).

Document the meeting, as this will help you with future coaching sessions.

QUICK REFERENCE CHECKLIST #4

Goal & Role Clarification

Have you:

* Helped the team members experience why they are to perform in a certain manner?

* Helped create links between individual, team, department and organizational goals?

* Articulated goals that are Measurable, Achievable, Realistic, and Controllable (M.A.R.C.)?

* Outlined tangible evidence that the goals have been met and, if not, provide appropriate coaching?

QUICK REFERENCE CHECKLIST #5

Coaching to Performance Goals

Have you:

* Described in detail the aspects of performance that need improvement?

* Indicated why the performance is of concern?

* Probed for reasons and listened openly to the explanation?

* Discussed specific actions to improve performance and how they must be implemented?

* Discussed and agreed upon when actions must be taken and appropriate follow-up date/s?

PROBLEM #3

	SYMPTOM	POSSIBLE CAUSE	SOLUTION
	3. When team consensus decision-making opportunities arise there is arguing, distrust and confusion resulting eventually in a "who cares" attitude.	Not truly understanding what consensus decision-making involves.	Discussion of what consensus decision-making is and how to achieve it.

Discussion of the Team Decision-Making Process

Depending upon the situation, Team Leaders might ask their team for input on decisions that will affect them. During the past 35 years, Team Leaders have been brainwashed by the horde of so-called management 'experts', to believe that the only way to make a decision that impacts their team, is to have the team come to a consensus on that decision. Any Team Leader knows that there are times when this decision-making style is quite appropriate — and other times where it is inappropriate and they should make the decisions themselves. Suffice to say that many teams will automatically believe that if a Team Leader asks for their help in a decision, then consensus will be the process used.

If a Team Leader decides that s/he would like to have the team make a decision through consensus, then it is crucial that the team understands what consensus decision-making entails. If for example, a Team Leader decides that his/her team should make a decision on production scheduling, he/she should outline the following:

A. The value of making decisions by consensus

B. What consensus means at an operational, practical level

C. What "givens" or organizational constraints are attached to the decision?

D. What will be the members' "fall-back" decision-making approach if they cannot reach a consensus?

A. The Value of Making Decisions by Consensus

The Team Leader will want to emphasize that the benefits and values of making a decision by consensus are:

✳ Increases involvement and participation by all team members.

✳ Equalizes the distribution of power.

✳ Increases team cohesion.

✳ Allows for shared risk and a willingness to adopt more extreme positions and creative solutions.

✳ Increases motivation to be involved and contribute.

✳ Tends to more readily change attitudes, opinions and behaviour.

✳ Provides time for constructive controversy and airing of diverse opinions.

✳ Improves the quality of decisions.

✳ Encourages confidence in the "correctness" of decisions.

✳ Increases commitment to implement decisions.

B. What Consensus Is

The Team Leader will want to explain what consensus actually looks like:

✱ Consensus is an agreement among team members to support each other for the common good; and can only occur when everyone has participated in the decision-making process that is worthwhile to everybody. Consensus means that even those who do not agree can at least support the group decision if only for a trial period. It means they are willing to buy into somebody else's risk for a period of time.

✱ Consensus is flexibility. The process of reaching consensus often uncovers thoughts and ideas that might otherwise not have emerged. Often the course of discussion is carried in other directions and a different; perhaps more creative, solution or decision is reached. Often teams find routes to agreements that nobody recognized at the outset.

✱ Consensus is finding accommodations, not necessarily compromises, for varying viewpoints. It requires exploring and thoroughly understanding all points of view. Decisions made by consensus tend to pull people together rather than polarizing them as voting and compromising often do.

What Consensus Is Not

The Team Leader will want to emphasize what consensus is not — so that there is no confusion amongst the team members:

✱ Consensus is not unanimous agreement. Since differing points of view are commonplace and more than one can be "right" at any point, unanimous agreement on topics of significance is an unusual phenomenon. When unanimous agreement is the written or unwritten rule of a team, differing views are often not expressed for fear of bucking a trend or delaying a decision.

✱ **Consensus does not mean saying "yes" when you really mean "no". Lack of commitment and follow-through are almost always the result when dissent is not expressed and fully discussed.**

✱ **Consensus is not a majority rule. When the minority is forced to go along with the majority, both subtle and overt resistance might occur. Primarily for this reason, voting to make decisions should be discouraged. While minority opinions will still exist in consensus decisions, the process requires a degree of discussion and interchange that often doesn't occur when voting is the rule.**

If for example, the definition of consensus is not discussed up front at the meeting around production scheduling, it has the potential to cause fireworks two or three hours into the meeting when all of a sudden the team is hit with "decision-making" time.

Comments will abound like "How are we making the decision? I assume consensus?!" Other people might say "Forget consensus, it should be majority rules." It is very difficult to have a productive discussion when emotions are high. *The five to ten minute investment upfront discussing what consensus is and is not will pay off dramatically in terms of both reducing the time to make the decisions and minimizing the emotional intensity.*

C. What "givens" or organizational constraints are attached to the decision?

A common error that many novice Team Leaders make when using a consensus approach to decision making is not laying out realistic boundaries or organizational constraints to the team before the process starts. With the absence of constraints, many well-intentioned teams will devise fantastic ideas only to have them labeled "unworkable" when they present such ideas to their Team Leader.

For example, the team that has been asked to work out a production schedule which must accommodate a three shift, 24-7 system, will require a list of givens or constraints that must be placed on their decisions.

Some of the givens in this situation might be:

✳ **Overtime must be kept at a minimum (e.g. no more than 2-3 hours per person)**
✳ **No individual can work more than 10 hours straight**
✳ **There must be adequate coverage between the critical times of 8:00 am and 4:30 pm**

Having these constraints in place avoids situations that will demotivate team members when all their hard work becomes obsolete, a result that leads to apathy toward future consensus decision-making opportunities.

As can be seen in Figure 3.4, a team has been asked to look at ways to make an office area more attractive to customers. On the left side of the chart you see the real organizational constraints, on the right side you see the self-imposed constraints. Note that the real organizational constraints are usually around budget, expenditure and staffing issues. It can be very challenging for the Team Leader to look at what true constraints are versus options that s/he just does

> **The challenge for the Team Leader is the ability to differentiate between real organizational constraints and his/her own self-imposed constraints.**

Real Organizational Constraints	Self-Imposed Constraints
* Budget limited to $100,000	* No artificial plants
* Accommodate two reception personnel	* "Open" concept
* Must stick with corporate "colours"	* Photographs on walls not paintings
* Must accommodate up to 5 guests	* Limited use of mirrors

Figure 3.4 Constraints Re: Making the Office Area More Attractive to Customers

not want to entertain as a possible solution. A Team Leader must have plenty of self-awareness in order to differentiate between the two. If too many self-imposed constraints are put on the team, as illustrated below, the team starts to question whether they truly have any influence on the decision.

Remember, the Team Leader has the right to make any decision that he or she deems appropriate — even if doing so means overriding the team's consensus. However, Team Leaders must also realize that the more often this is done, the less motivated the team becomes when asked to make future decisions by consensus.

D. What will be the members' "fallback" decision-making approach if they cannot reach consensus?

There is a fair amount of controversy around whether you actually want to provide a team with a fallback decision-making approach if consensus cannot be reached. The controversy stems from the theory that if the team believes there might be an easier way to make a decision then they will take the path of least resistance and conveniently find a way not to reach consensus.

My experience has shown that this might be the case with reasonably new teams or dysfunctional teams — however, if a team is solidly grounded and understands its goals, roles and procedures (See Chapter 1) then they will be motivated to reach most decisions by consensus — if they are unable to reach consensus, most high performance teams will see this as a failure. High performance teams will more likely see the decision as a team challenge and strive to meet that challenge rather than reverting to another fall-back decision making style.

My advice to Team Leaders is that there is only one fallback decision-making approach – namely, letting the team know that you will take back the accountability for the decision personally.

This is not articulated as a threat but as the reality of having to make a timely business decision. Also remember that as Team Leader you never truly gave up the accountability for the decisions from an

QUICK REFERENCE CHECKLIST #6

Consensus Decision Making

Have you discussed:

* The value of making decisions by consensus

* What consensus is?

* What consensus is not?

* What "givens" or organizational constraints are attached to the decision?

* What will be the members' "fallback" decision-making approach if they cannot reach a consensus?

organizational perspective — in essence you delegated that accountability to the team. My experience has shown that if the Team Leader does an appropriate job up-front — explaining the organizational constraints, facilitating the creation of ground rules and communication channels — that very few teams, whether they be experienced or not, will need to defer to the Team Leader to make the decision for them.

Problem #4

	SYMPTOM	POSSIBLE CAUSE	SOLUTION
	4. Inappropriate or inadequate communication amongst team members and/or Team Leader.	Team members do not understand the why's and how's behind inter-team communications.	Discussion of the appropriate type of communication media and strategies when and how to use them .

Discussion of the Team's Communication Channels

In every organization, each team will have a preferred method or process by which they communicate. Some teams will exclusively use e-mail, others will use the telephone, others will have face-to-face meetings, and many teams will use a combination of all three. *Therefore, it is critical that the Team Leader, in conjunction with the team members work out a system that will allow them to communicate, not only with each other, on a daily basis, but also with the Team Leader and the organization as a whole.*

Chapter 2 of this book deals with the communications strategies that need to be employed during team meetings and discussions. An entire book can be devoted to the intricacies of team communications, however the focus in this section is limited to two specific areas: the use and abuse of email, and the process by which team members should be communicating vital information upwards to you, the Team Leader. My experience has shown that these two aspects of inter-team communication are easy targets for improvement involving a minimal amount of time and training on the part of the Team Leader.

Communicating Via E-mail[14]

E-mail has become the prevalent mode of communication not only amongst teams but also in every aspect of day-to-day communication both in our business and personal lives.

Although e-mail is quick and convenient it is not always the best means of team communication.

Opt for a telephone call or face-to-face meeting if the following circumstances apply:

* Your message is extremely important or confidential, and you can't risk an invasion of privacy. If you are not comfortable with the possibility of having your words read by an unintended audience, don't use e-mail.

* You need to deliver unpopular news and don't want to appear cold or indifferent. Deliver bad news in person or via the telephone; this gives you the opportunity to expand on your message with appropriate facial expressions, body language and vocal inflection – the human touch. For example, e-mail would be the most effective way to notify the Customer Service Team of a mandatory team meeting. But the meeting itself - not an impersonal e-mail message - would be the appropriate place to break the news that the team is being downsized.

14. Partially based on excerpts from "Writing Effective E-Mail", Nancy Flynn and Tom Flynn 1998.

* There is a chance that the intent of your e-mail message will be lost in translation. Subtle nuances in tone are hard to pick up on in an email format. For example, receiving an email from another team member that you respect that reads "You will need to do X and Y before month end..." will be viewed as a simple request. The same request all of a sudden takes on a negative connation and becomes a demand if it is written by a team member with whom you have a history of conflict.

* You need an immediate response. E-mail might be the best way to deliver news fast, but it is not necessarily the best route to a quick reply. For an immediate response to a pressing team issue or question, use the telephone or meet face-to-face.

* When you are frustrated and upset with a specific team member or the team itself. Count to ten before you hit that send button!! Once that damaging message is sent it is difficult, if not impossible to retract.

Before you write your first electronic word, consider your message and your intended reader. Acknowledge and consider any outside factors, such as language barriers, time zone differences and "hidden" readers, all of which could affect how your electronic message is received. Then decide whether or not e-mail is the appropriate medium or not.

Tips on Writing Effective E-mail Both Inter-Team and Intra-Team

1. Be Reader-Centered. Write specifically, even technically, if the situation calls for it; but always provide a brief executive summary at the beginning of the document. The summary serves two purposes:

* Any team member, regardless of background, will understand your message.

*   Because the summary is written in conversational language and appears at the beginning of the document, you stand a better chance of maintaining the interest of a team member who might not have the inclination to work through a complex, technical document.

2. Use the Subject Line Appropriately. Be specific about what is included in the body of the message. "Action Items for February 7th Team Meeting" is much more informative than "Upcoming Meeting." Furthermore if you tend to save and categorize emails by subject for future reference this makes the cataloging process that much simpler.

3. Keep an Eye on Spelling, Grammar and Punctuation. You can be sure your team members will notice even if you don't.

4. Don't Negotiate Through E-mail. When you are negotiating a schedule change that will affect your team members, e-mail is not the medium for the actual negotiation. Unless you are a prolific writer, e-mail lacks the subtle nuances on which face-to-face, or voice-to-voice negotiations are built. Negotiations by e-mail have the distinction of being the most misconstrued, anger-inducing medium available to us.

Use face-to-face discussions when negotiating with team members; use e-mail to document what was agreed upon and follow-up actions that must occur to support the negotiations.

Coaching Team Members to Effectively Communicate Upward

"The frustration experienced by team members as they try to communicate an item of importance to a Team Leader is only outweighed by the frustration of a Team Leader who is the recipient of the communication".

Tony White quoting every Team Leader and team member
with whom he has ever worked.

> Most Team Leaders don't understand that, from a team member's perspective, communicating upwards can be both intimidating and frustrating.

In my training business I have had the opportunity to work with the entire organizational hierarchy ranging from the front-line worker to the CEO. If I had one dollar for every time that I heard, from every level of personnel, "I just wish they would communicate better to me", I would be writing this book from my multi million-dollar condo in the south of France. However, as I am writing from the confines of my southern Ontario home, on a bone chilling day in February, let me say that astute Team Leaders need to realize the importance of clear, concise and on-going communication between themselves and their team members.

The most effective Team Leaders spend time instructing their members on the best way to frame their messages in order to get the Team Leaders' undivided attention.

The following four-step communication process should be taught to your team members, especially if you perceive that they are either reticent or are having difficulty communicating important issues to you.

Steps to Hit Your Team Leader's Priority List- Communicating Vital News Upward

1. Frame the situation appropriately, through your Team Leader's eyes

* What information will your Team Leader need in order to assist you with your situation? Will s/he need reports, statistics or any other "objective" information; and, is it easily accessible? Avoid going into the meeting with only hunches, intuitions and "gut" feelings.

* Can the situation be framed into something that keeps your Team Leader awake at night? In other words, if quality issues are presently on the Team Leader's mind, can you ensure that your issue directly or at least indirectly, relates to quality issues?

2. Detail the implications of the current situation on both your team and the organization

* To further capture their interest, give a brief, detailed description on how the issue, if not dealt with correctly, will impact both the team and the organization "This really screws up our team," has little impact compared to, "The specs for XYZ program seem to be off by 10 percent – if we can't find out the source of this error by Friday, the team will be forced to shut down the line which will end up costing us more than $10,000.00."

3. Have a proposed solution and action plan prepared

* Nothing will infuriate a Team Leader more than a list of the issues without any potential solutions – the issues now become other tasks that the Team Leader must add to his/her list and one more reason why the team member begins to look more and more expendable!

* Detailing one or more options, including both the pros and cons of each re: cost, time, resources and the likelihood of acceptance by the team or organization, etc., is critical if you truly want the Team Leader to take your ideas seriously.

4. Ask for input/advice

* This is probably where most team members start and end the communication process. The bottom-line is that you are still coming to the Team Leader for information and/or advice on an issue. If you carry out the previous three steps, then:

* Actually hitting his/her priority list increases dramatically

* The perception of you as an excellent communicator increases

* You reduce the chances of conflict

Summary

This chapter has examined some of the most common reasons why teams run into trouble and outlined the skills and strategies required by the Team Leader to get the team back on track. Although there can be many root causes for a team that is not performing to its expected level, my experience leads me to believe that goal and role confusion, the inability to use consensus effectively, not communicating appropriately or efficiently and lack of behavioural guidelines are the most likely causes.

The Team Leader, by examining the symptoms as outlined, and then systematically working through the coaching and instructional tools presented in this chapter, should observe an increased commitment and collective competence in his/her team as well as higher levels of drive and job satisfaction.

4 Final Thoughts

I was asked recently by a Team Leader, in a workshop that I was running at a large pharmaceutical company in Toronto, the following question:

"Tony, if there was *only one thing that I could do on a regular basis* with my team to be a more effective Team Leader, what would it be?"

The question gave me pause for thought, as there are so many things that a Team Leader should be doing, as detailed in this book, and trying to narrow it down to one specific thing was challenging to say the least.

After a few seconds I said, "Have a plan", which was followed up with the Team Leader asking me "What sort of plan, specifically?"

Let me explain what I mean by "having a plan…".

Today, Team Leaders operate in a very different environment than they did 25 years ago. They probably weren't called Team Leaders;

they were called supervisors or managers. With the advent of a more team-oriented approach to management over the past three decades, these supervisors were now expected, overnight, to become Team Leaders —usually without any additional training or coaching on how to be successful as Team Leaders. I have worked with dozens of people who have said to me that they are Team Leaders in name only — nothing has changed from the days when they were known as supervisors or managers. Is it any wonder that many of these Team Leaders struggle on a daily basis with their responsibilities when they have not had the appropriate guidance from their managers?

Most Team Leaders know how to plan – they plan budgets, work schedules, job coverage, equipment maintenance to name just a few. *Team Leaders of high performance teams also plan how to lead and motivate a team.* As you read this book you noticed that there are many small details that need to be planned before entering into a meeting, for example, with your team members. Are you planning to run a tightly controlled discussion or an open discussion? Are you going to ask the team to help you make a decision through consensus or are you going to make the decision yourself? Are you going to use a "scenario" question to engage your team in problem solving or an "experience" question? These are just a few of the questions that you can now intelligently answer after reading this book. However, if you have not formally planned how and when to implement these techniques, they become "nice to do's" not "need to do's" and honestly, given today's time constraints, they drop to the very bottom of your priority list and are eventually forgotten.

The tips and techniques are not difficult to carry out with your team.

As I say to participants of my workshops, now you can be effective as a Team Leader by design, not default— *in other words, you can now plan for your success as a Team Leader rather than learning it the hard way, through trial and error.*

To help you plan for the implementation of the key strategies and skills required to be a leader of a high-performance team, I have included Quick Reference Checklists throughout the book. Photocopy the pages or cut them out and post them in an area that is easily accessible and user-friendly.

Best of luck with your journey!

Book Order Form

To order extra copies of **Make it Happen: A Practical Handbook for Team Leaders, Project Managers and Facilitators to Build, Facilitate and Repair High-Performance Teams,** send the clip-out below and enclose either a personal cheque or money order (do not send cash) made payable to:

Tony White
103 Pinnacle Trail
Aurora, Ontario, Canada
L4G 7G7

Phone: 905. 713. 2638
Fax: 905. 841. 3074
Email: tonyw@aci.on.ca

Please tear off and include:

Name: _____

Address: _____

_____

_____

City:_____ Prov./State: _____

PC/Zip: _____ Country_____

Email: _____

____ copies of **Make it Happen** x $24.95 CAD

Canadian orders please include 7% GST and **$4.00** for shipping and handling.
US orders $19.95 US plus applicable taxes and **$6.00** for shipping and handling.
UK orders £9.95 plus applicable taxes and **£5.00** for shipping and handling.

Orders for more than 3 books, or other international orders, please call or e-mail us and we will assist you with a price reduction based on the volume of your order.

Total Payment enclosed: $ _____ by cheque/money order

Please allow 4-6 weeks for delivery

Tony's Training Philosophy

Whereas "soft skills" may conjure up images of "nice skills" nothing could be further from the truth. Soft skills are not "warm and fuzzies"- they are *core competencies* that when demonstrated consistently with both staff and clients can mean the difference between professional *success and failure.*

In modern-day business soft skills are a hard reality™

Tony has been referred to as the *"Soft Skill Specialist"* as he speaks and consults on over twelve disciplines ranging from communication and team leadership to facilitation and negotiation skills.

When competition is stiff, your organizations collective soft skill competence can become your biggest competitive advantage in the market place.

Experience

When it comes to experience with diverse industries as well as different levels in the organizational hierarchy, *Tony's experience is hard to beat.*

It is estimated that he has worked with over 500 private and 300 public sector clients in the past twenty years encompassing over 10,000 participants.

"Energizing, Practical & Relevant"……..

Words often used to describe a keynote address or workshop by Tony White (M.A.). He has facilitated training workshops and delivered keynote addresses for a broad cross section of business, education and government organizations for close to twenty years.

Whether he is one mile underground in Northern Manitoba teaching gold miners how to train, or facilitating a collaborative sales discussion between two CEOs of international companies in downtown Manhattan, Tony does it *knowledgeably, practically and collaboratively.*

The unique ability to build rapport immediately with anyone in an organization from the front-line team members to the CEO, allows him to break down any barriers quickly and to do what he does best-*communicate, motivate and get others to participate.*

Affiliations

As well as running his own training and development company www.tonywhitetraining.com Tony is a Senior Consultant with Practical Management Inc., a 40 year old training & development company in Nevada, USA.

Furthermore, Tony is a part-time faculty member at the University of Toronto, Faculty of Applied Science & Engineering in Toronto, Ontario, Canada.

Providing Exceptional Customer Service

Tony spends the time upfront to listen and understand exactly what your training or presentation needs are. He takes his vast amount of experience over the past twenty years to customize a refined presentation or workshop that targets the specific needs of your group. No filler, no fads no "flavor of the month" - only information that inspires, motivates and is relevant to personal & professional success!

How to Reach Tony

E-mail: tonyw@aci.on.ca

Web: www.tonywhitetraining.com

Mailing Address:
103 Pinnacle Trail
Aurora, Ontario, Canada
L4G 7G7

Phone: 905-713-2638
Fax: 905-841-3074